"A finely told coming-of-age story th[...]
father and son, a bond strengthened through the love of sports."
— *Detroit Free Press*

"Will resonate with any of us who ever sat in the stands to watch our sons play high school sports . . . pick it up, and share in the maddening magic of living with a teenager."
— *St. Louis Post-Dispatch*

"Here is a book that should be read by the parents of teenagers and the teenagers themselves. It is about baseball, but so much more than baseball at the same time. It is about fathers and sons, about memory and dreams, about growing up and growing older, about letting go. Finally, it is about how fast childhood goes, for all of us."
— Mike Lupica, author of *Travel Team* and *Heat*

"This season's best entry in the rich vein of stories about fathers and sons and baseball."
— *Seattle Post-Intelligencer*

"In a most entertaining way, Dan Shaughnessy has shared with us the joys and responsibilities of raising a son different from himself."
— Lesley Visser, CBS sportscaster

"Perhaps the best book Shaughnessy has written to date . . . a book that is noteworthy in its candor, and a well-written volume to be savored."
— *Nantucket Independent*

"I love this book. Truth and common sense jump from the printed page. If you've ever been a father, standing on the sidelines, watching your child play youth sports, a stew of doubts, anxieties, memories, and epiphanies swirling in your head, you'll wish you were standing next to Dan Shaughnessy. He tells you that you're not alone."
— Leigh Montville, author of *Ted Williams* and *The Big Bam*

"Part love song to baseball, part autobiography, part a recounting of his son's senior year in high school, this book delivers its tributes elegantly."
— *Library Journal*, starred review

"It's in the smaller moments that *Senior Year* is most triumphant."
— *Boston Magazine*

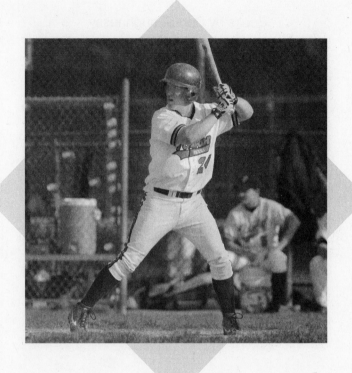

Books by Dan Shaughnessy

Courtside
(with Gary Hoenig)

One Strike Away

The Curse of the Bambino

Ever Green:
The Boston Celtics

Seeing Red:
The Red Auerbach Story

At Fenway

Fenway
(with Stan Grossfeld)

Spring Training
(with Stan Grossfeld)

The Legend of the
Curse of the Bambino

Reversing the Curse

Senior Year

SENIOR YEAR

A Father, a Son,
and
High School Baseball

Dan Shaughnessy

A Mariner Book
Houghton Mifflin Company
BOSTON · NEW YORK

First Mariner Books edition 2008

Copyright © 2007 by Dan Shaughnessy

www.houghtonmifflinbooks.com

Library of Congress Cataloging-in-Publication Data
Shaughnessy, Dan.
Senior year : a father, a son, and high school baseball
/ Dan Shaughnessy.
p. cm.
ISBN-13: 978-0-618-72905-0
ISBN-10: 0-618-72905-4
1. Baseball—Miscellanea. 2. Shaughnessy, Dan.
3. Fathers and sons. I. Title.
GV867.3.S53 2007
796.357'62—dc22   2006030477

ISBN 978-0-547-05382-0 (pbk.)

Book design by Melissa Lotfy

Printed in the United States of America

VB 10 9 8 7 6 5 4 3 2 1

Frontispiece: (left) Dan Shaughnessy, pitching at
Groton High School, 1968; (right) Sam Shaughnessy,
hitting at Newton North High School, 2006.

To:

♦

JOHN P. FAHEY
ANDRE VAN HOOGEN
JOHN COLANTONIO
JOE KING
MANNY CONNERNEY
JOE SICILIANO

♦

And all those who coach and
teach our children . . .

Contents

SENIOR YEAR

◆

SENIOR YEAR

Introduction

IT WAS GETTING DARK and I was standing in the parking lot beyond the right field fence at the high school baseball field. The kids call it "third lot." It once provided parking for Newton North High School students, but that was before too many kids got cars, so now it's reserved for faculty and seniors during school hours. At this moment, third lot was two-thirds empty and the only remaining cars belonged to the players on the baseball team, plus a handful of parents and friends.

I had my keys in my hand. I'd already said goodbye to my old high school coach, who'd made the drive down from New Hampshire to sit with me and watch my son play. It was a cold New England May day and the game was running long and I had to get going. I was due at a wake for the 21-year-old son of my cousin. The wake was taking place in the small town where I was born, an hour's drive to the west, and the notice in the newspaper said visiting hours would be over at 7 P.M.

It had been an emotional day, sitting on the cold metal slats, watching Sam hit, catching up with my old coach, and thinking about what my cousin Mickey was going through. I hadn't seen Mickey in over a year. We were never especially close. That happens when you have fifty-one first cousins and move away after college. But it was easy to remember everything I admired about Mickey. He was a terrific high school athlete, only two years older than me. He seemed to be better than everyone else at everything: Football. Basketball. Skiing. He was strong, tough, skilled, and movie-star handsome. He had his own rock 'n' roll band. Chicks dug him and guys wanted to be him. It would have been easy to hate the guy, but he was generous and caring, and when I would see him years later he was always humble about his high school greatness. He'd made a fine life for himself, working for the gas company and raising two kids with his wife. Now he was getting ready to bury his son, young Michael, who had died at home in bed, another victim of the national scourge of Oxycontin. Michael had been a high school football stud, just like his father. He had been good enough to win a scholarship to Wagner College, and there had been a picture in the local newspaper of Michael signing his letter of intent. Now, just a couple of years later, his picture was in the paper again, accompanied by one of those impossibly sad stories about a promising young life that ended too soon.

So I was feeling a little guilty as I stood in third lot, jangling my keys and watching the high school baseball game groan into extra innings. I didn't want to miss the wake, but I remembered that earlier in the day Mickey's brother had told me, "We'll be there long after seven." Besides, Sam was scheduled to lead off the bottom of the tenth and he was due. He had been hitting the ball hard all day, but he was sitting on an 0-4 and I knew his small world would tumble into chaos and panic if he went hitless for the day. Such is the fragility and self-absorption of the high school mind.

I was wondering about my own mind, too. I am a professional sportswriter, specializing in baseball. I've been a columnist for the *Boston Globe* for more than fifteen years, covering Olympics, Super Bowls, World Series, Stanley Cup Finals, NBA Championships, and Ryder Cups. I traveled with the Baltimore Orioles,

Boston Celtics, and Red Sox back in the days when writers really traveled and lived with the ballplayers. I've written ten books, seven on baseball. I can go to any game, any time I want. And yet I find myself fixated on the successes and failures of Newton North High School and Sam Shaughnessy, my only son and the youngest of three ballplaying children. Sam's sisters had fun and fulfilling seasons in high school volleyball, field hockey, and softball, and I was amazed at how following their games connected me to their school and our community while kindling so many thoughts of my own high school days thirty years earlier. Probably that's why I found myself suddenly skipping Red Sox road trips and canceling TV appearances because of weather-forced changes in the high school baseball season. Random Sox fans wanted to ask me about Curt Schilling and Jonathan Papelbon. I'd rather talk about Newton North lefthander, J. T. Ross.

The score was still tied when Sam walked to the plate to open up the bottom of the tenth, and we were definitely losing the light, making it even tougher to hit. The Braintree coach came out to talk to his pitcher. I looked at the sky. I looked at my watch. This was it. I'd stare through the chain link for one more at bat, then get in the car. Darkness was going to make this the last inning, even if the score was still tied after ten.

And then, in an instant, the baseball was screeching over the first baseman's head, over the rightfielder's head, over the chain link, and onto the trunk of the 1998 Toyota Corolla that Sam had driven to school that day. It rolled across the lot and came to rest under a tree. I retrieved the ball while he circled the bases.

There was no such thing as a "walkoff" home run when I went to high school. We had read the stories about Bobby Thomson's Shot Heard Round the World, and all my friends and I knew that the Pirates' second baseman Bill Mazeroski had won the 1960 World Series with a homer in the bottom of the ninth . . . but nobody talked about "walkoffs" until Kirk Gibson dropped one on Dennis Eckersley in the 1988 World Series. Eck popularized the term, and now there are walkoff homers, walkoff doubles, walkoff walks, even an occasional walkoff balk.

In any event, Sam Shaughnessy had his first high school walk-off homer (a drive-off walkoff, given the dent in the Toyota) and knew enough to take his helmet off after rounding third base. He had seen Red Sox slugger David Ortiz do this a lot. A helmetless head is less likely to be pounded by your teammates.

I walked in from right field and delivered the baseball to my smiling son. I told him not to worry about the dent on the roof of the trunk (not sure my dad would have been so casual about the damage done). Then I got in my car and drove to the wake.

The country roads took me back. They took me to the place where I grew up, the place where I experienced all the highs and lows that were now happening to Sam. I remembered how it felt to have a moment like he had today, and I knew he would hold it in his heart for the rest of his life. Sports have a way of defining our lives, particularly teenage lives. The local high school basketball games were a big deal in my hometown when I was growing up. Most of our parents came to the games and sat in the back row of the small gym. The successes and failures of our team made for conversation around the post office and drug store in the center of town. We connected through sports.

Two decades later, when my classmates filled out a reunion form, there was a question regarding your favorite high school memory. I was struck by how many answered "Dances after the Friday night basketball games." These were not just the ball-players and cheerleaders. These were kids who had never played on the team, but as grownups they had fond memories of cold nights in a warm gym, when a sporting event was the center of our tiny universe.

The trick is to keep moving forward and not let the glory days of high school become the highlight of your life.

When I wheeled into the funeral home a few minutes after seven, there was a line the length of a football field waiting to pay respects to Michael. Inside, I joined my sisters, cousins, aunts, and uncles and waited for the line to dwindle. In my mind, I pledged not to speak of why I was late or of how the game had ended.

A couple of hours later, the line completely exhausted, I knelt before young Michael and said a prayer. Inside the open casket, there was a photo of Michael celebrating a high school football victory with his teammates. When I stood up, cousin Mickey was there, sobbing, spent, but still strong enough to hug me with the force of a linebacker.

It is a universal truth that it's virtually impossible to say anything appropriate in a moment like this. Nothing is worse than a parent losing a child. The loss is unspeakable and incomprehensible. Only those who have experienced such a tragedy can possibly know what it feels like. But the events of my day had given me special perspective, and for once I felt like I knew exactly what to say.

"Michael must have given you a lot of joy."

"Oh, Danny," he said, smiling through the tears, pointing to the photo inside the casket. "You should have seen him play. And not just because he was my son, either. That was the Acton-Boxboro game. One of the greatest nights for all of them. I loved watching him play more than anything."

There it was. I knew then I had made the right decision, staying an extra inning to see the end of a high school baseball game while my sisters and cousins and aunts and uncles were already at the wake. And as I drove home, back across the roads of my youth, I knew I had to write something down.

Groton to Newton

I T'S EMBARRASSING TO ADMIT, but I kept a diary in high school. Such a dork. Today, a teenager might get away with calling it a "journal," but only cheerleaders and pretty-in-pink girls keep a locked book under the bed and begin each entry with "Dear Diary." Naturally, I still have the two small books (covering junior and senior years), and it's hilarious to read through the well-worn pages. I have a 35-year-old niece who was born during my senior year of high school, and during a recent holiday gathering, I fetched the book to see what I had written on the day after she was born. And there it was. After several paragraphs about sitting next to Eleanor Lehtinen in study hall, and getting a pimple on my nose, and Friday night's big win over Nashoba Regional, there was a single closing line that read, "Mary had a baby girl last night."

In *The Rise and Fall of the American Teenager,* Thomas Hine wrote, "Figuring out where they fit in—to the universe, the economy, their social circle, their family—is a project on which teenagers spend a lot of their time and energy."

That, and looking in the mirror and thinking about the next game, of course.

My hideous, humble journal serves as a reminder of how immature and insecure one can be at the age of 18. Looking back,

I'm amazed how busy and needy I was in those final days of high school. But I don't need the diary to remember what it felt like when the next game was the most important event in my life. There's an 18-year-old forever locked away inside all of us; that's why you'll always see balding men with big bellies driving sports cars, buying young women drinks, and pulling hamstrings playing full court basketball.

The joy of playing ball never leaves us. If you have hit a baseball over a fence or finished first in a race or even just sat on the bench—satisfied to be a part of something with your friends —you never forget the feeling. It starts the first time we kick a ball into a goal or beat our sister in a footrace when we are 4 years old. It might be in a backyard, on a beach, or in an asphalt alley behind a three-decker house. You don't have to be on *Wide World of Sports* to experience "the thrill of victory and the agony of defeat": it happens in your earliest days of dodge ball. Not everyone plays the piano or violin, but just about every kid boots a soccer ball and runs a race. Fortunate fathers and moms get a second go-around. Watching a child pass through the same passages connects every parent to his or her own youth.

I had the good fortune to be born in Groton, Massachusetts, in 1953, the youngest of Bill and Eileen Shaughnessy's five children. Bill was a sales executive at a bag company, a particularly boring and low-paying job. Eileen was a nurse. They met when he had his appendix removed at Cambridge City Hospital, where she worked. Family folklore holds that Mom and Dad's first date was a wake somewhere far north in Maine. My father had been pestering the pretty young nurse for a date, but she informed him that she didn't go out with patients. He persisted. She finally caved in, but only because she needed a ride to the wake of one of her roommate's parents. Way to go, Dad. Sounds like the definition of desperation.

My father was a smart, handsome man. He had attended Boston College, where he matriculated with Thomas "Tip" O'Neill, later the longtime speaker of the U.S. House of Representatives. It turned out that the Shaughnessys had at one time rented from the O'Neills in Cambridge, and my dad liked to dismiss the great speaker by informing us, "I put the bum through college."

My dad's brother claims Bill Shaughnessy was quite the sportsman in his youth, but by the time I came along, Dad wasn't moving much, unless he was picking up sticks and stones in our rather large backyard (our twelve-room farmhouse was purchased for $7,000 with help from the GI Bill one year after Dad came home from Germany). Dad was thirty-nine years older than me and I never saw him run. We never played catch or did anything athletic together. I guess that's what friends and older siblings were for. This was the 1950s and '60s, and fathers dressed like Ward Cleaver. Bill Shaughnessy wore white shirts and black shoes every day of his working life. He did a little yard work around the house, but that was it. There was one day when he came home from work and found me by the side door with a baseball bat in my hands, and for some reason he decided to offer a little instruction. He told me that he had been a pretty fair power hitter in his day and that he'd once scattered some local girls with one of his prodigious blasts off a park bench. Then he proceeded to demonstrate how he would walk into the pitch as it was coming toward home plate—for additional power. I was only 10 years old, but I knew that was dopey. I thanked him for the ridiculous hitting lesson and watched him go inside where he'd sit in his brown Archie Bunker chair, read his paper, and maybe wind down with a highball before dinner.

My dad never made much money, but somehow kept things afloat and managed to send all five kids off to college. He was a master money manager; we were so frugal we stripped tinsel off the Christmas tree and used it again the following year. When I was in high school, and the other four kids were gone—one still in college—Dad borrowed money from me. My diary entries are quite clear on this. Dad borrowed $250 of the dough I'd saved from working as a soda jerk at the local ice cream and fried clam joint, Johnson's Drive-In. Two-fifty was a fortune in 1970. Minimum wage was $1.60 per hour and making seventy-five cents in tips in one shift was noteworthy in my daily log.

Poring through the pages of my tattered journals, I am struck by how many of the daily entries began with "Dad and I went to the dump this morning." Apparently that was how we bonded. We would load up the trunk of Dad's four-door Ford sedan and off to the dump we'd go, toting bags of papers and trash (coffee grounds, eggshells, and other perishables were discarded in separate barrels and left on the curb to be taken to local pig farms). Dad spilled a lot of wisdom on those dump runs, but I cannot remember much of what was said. The conversation I remember best came in November 1963, when we drove to the dump on a rainy Saturday, the day after our president was assassinated, and he told me that people would be talking about this for the rest of my life. He saved the sex talk for a day when he was driving me to the orthodontist (I was 14!). The dump run was for talking about school and sports and family issues. There are no dumps anymore, only "landfills." Sadly, my kids have never been to a landfill. Or a dump. I have had to find alternative locations for heart-to-heart, dad-to-kid chats.

My mom was even less athletic than my dad. She was a stunning, strong woman who had helped raise her seven siblings (six brothers), making lunches, scrubbing piles of laundry, ironing everything (even socks and underwear), and washing dirty dishes by hand. When she became a wife and mother, it was more of the same. We never had a mechanical dishwasher or clothes dryer. My siblings and I share goofy winter memories of bringing frozen sheets and T-shirts in from the clothesline. We called them "the boards."

Mom would have been a perfect politician's wife. She was fastidious about remembering names and writing thank-you notes. She had great posture (her college yearbook declared that her favorite sport was "standing erect") and the best penmanship of anyone I have ever known. She could not afford luxury items, but she always insisted on quality. That went for us, too, when it came to buying shoes or sports coats. We didn't have many extras, but the stuff we had was top shelf. For all of her hard work —chores that made her hands rougher than she would have liked—Mom was something of a diva. No housecoats or curlers in *her* hair when she went out of the house. On beach outings, when it was time to leave, she made us fetch pails of water so she could wash the sand off her feet before putting on her shoes. The one-time Miss Silver Laker was ever dolled up, even when doing housework. She lived to be 81 years old, and not once did I ever see her with her hair wet or unkempt. Needless to say, I never saw her run, either.

Groton in the 1950s was something right out of a Ron Howard movie. The first play I saw in high school was Thornton Wilder's *Our Town,* and it struck me as totally boring and unremarkable because it depicted conversations and situations I heard and saw every day. Nothing special about that, right? Ours was a town of Yankee farmers who said little and wanted no one to know how much money and land they had. We never locked our doors and dialed only five numbers to make phone calls. Everyone knew everyone else's business, even when the days of the telephone party lines ended. My wife, Marilou, a native of Detroit, would be perplexed and charmed by this when she made her first trip to Groton in 1980. We stopped at Forcino's Market to pick up some groceries to bring home to my mother. As Leo Forcino was ringing up our purchases in his bloodstained apron (Leo was also the butcher, of course), he stopped, held aloft a half gallon of ice cream, and said, "Dan, you might not want this because your mother was in this morning and picked up some ice cream."

"Chocolate chip?" I asked.

"Yeah, chocolate chip, Dan," said Leo.

A half mile down the road, closer to home, we stopped at the town hardware store because Marilou needed double-A batteries for the flash on her camera. I stayed in the car and told her to ask for either of the Sargent brothers. My old schoolmates, Dana and Rickey Sargent, ran the store. She picked up a four-pack of Duracells and as Rickey was ringing up the purchase, she made an offhand remark about how wasteful it was to have to buy four batteries when you need only two. Invariably, the other two batteries get lost and go to waste. Hearing this, old Rick ripped open the package and sold her two of the batteries for half of the sticker price. Marilou was slapping her forehead and laughing when she got back to the car.

"What's up with this place?" she asked before relaying the story. Stuff like that never happened in Detroit.

For many years, there were no stoplights in Groton (one was grudgingly installed for the new millennium). It was a town of 4,000 in the 1950s, and I went to school with kids who lived on apple, dairy, and produce farms. Houses were far apart and we rode our bikes everywhere, sometimes lining our wheel spokes with baseball cards because we liked the way it sounded. An odd little man named Bravel Goulart cut our hair and would give me a nickel to go next door to Bruce Pharmacy and fetch a newspaper. Old school. Bravel cut our hair the way our dads and moms wanted it cut, even after the Beatles splashed ashore in 1964.

In this vast space of small-town serenity, it was baseball that filled the long summer days. And it was major league baseball that made us feel connected to something bigger than Groton. The Boston Red Sox weren't very good for most of the 1950s and '60s, but they always had a lot of home run hitters and every now and then someone would pitch a no-hitter. A huge relief pitcher named Dick Radatz entertained us by raising his arms over his head when he walked off the hill after fanning the great Mickey Mantle. We got to listen to the greatest announcer of them all, Curt Gowdy, and most of the weekend games were on TV. The Sox were the big league team in the big city. They were ours, even if they stunk. (Nobody ever said "sucks" in the 1960s, at least not without punishment. "Sucks" is, in fact, the new "stinks.") They lost more than they won, but we followed them anyway.

My first trip to a Red Sox game was in 1961, a weeknight win over the Orioles. Today, I silently curse my deceased parents for not getting to Fenway one year earlier. Ted Williams retired in 1960 and I never saw him play. His was a magical name in every New England home when I was a kid, but my folks did not think to get Danny to Fenway before Ted hung 'em up. So I went in 1961, in the second grade, and I remember that famous first glimpse of the Fenway green when I walked up the ramp with my dad and brother. Fenway was grainy, small, and gray on the tiny black-and-white Philco at home. Like most people my age, when I finally walked into that ancient yard for the first time, I was awed, overwhelmed, and tangled up in green. Unfortunately, I was not struck by the sight of Ted Williams taking batting practice, so I settled for a rookie leftfielder named Carl Yastrzemski. The Red Sox beat the Orioles that night, and I fell asleep in the back seat on the ride home. I was still one year removed from a lifetime's immersion in baseball.

It happened in the summer of 1962. Something just clicked. My older brother, Bill, was a local teen baseball sensation by the time I was 8, and no doubt this had much to do with my sudden fascination for all things baseball. I knew every player on every major league team. I collected baseball cards and baseball coins and watched every game that was on television. The '62 Sox were dreadful, but that hardly mattered. My world was baseball, and

I would play imaginary games with a rubber ball and my S & H Greenstamp/Tito Francona–model glove. We got our mail at the post office, and I faithfully stalked the brick building when my monthly *Sport* magazine was due. *Sport* featured a few too many stories about Mantle and Whitey Ford for my liking, but it didn't really matter much as long as it was baseball. The town librarian learned to set aside any new young-reader baseball novels. I'd inhale the cliché-laden texts and return them in a matter of days. I invented a baseball dice game and played an entire 162-game season with my imaginary teams. I wallpapered my bedroom with baseball photographs and played some form of baseball—often by myself—from the time I woke up until the sun went down, unless of course there was school or a family function. My sisters still laugh recalling my narration of imaginary games with a rubber ball at the back porch steps. They would chuckle while they dried dishes at the kitchen sink. Joan, who is ten years older than me, claims I would sometimes work myself into a fit of tears while playing one-on-one with myself. "Why didn't you just let yourself win?" she would later ask.

It was not that simple, of course, but how could anyone else understand the game inside my head? I was an 8-year-old baseball Rain Man.

In Billy Crystal's *City Slickers*, a female character teases three 40-year-old guys regarding their lack of intellectual curiosity contrasted with their remembrance of everything having to do with baseball. When she says, "I don't remember who played third base for Pittsburgh in 1960," all three simultaneously say, "Don Hoak."

Alone in the theater, I, too, stared at the screen and said, "Don Hoak."

I remember my uncle Chappy looking at the scorebook I kept while watching the 1964 World Series on television (Cardinals over the Yankees, 4–3) and telling me, "This is good. You should keep doing this. You might be able to do something with it."

Uncle Chappy was probably into his third whiskey by then. I'm sure he never remembered the conversation. But I did. And he was right.

As a professional baseball writer for more than thirty years, I've learned that many of the best big league players know little about players who came before them. It seems that the gifted ones are rarely devoted fans of the game. They're just really good at it. Nomar Garciaparra didn't waste any time memorizing the lineup of the 1982 California Angels. He was busy playing soccer and baseball better than the rest of his friends. In my experience, people who love baseball the most are often one step removed from the dugouts and bullpens. Fans, writers, broadcasters, and professional baseball executives get into the game because they love baseball. A lot of players get into it because they are good at it and it pays well. In the spring of 2006, Red Sox reliever Keith Foulke, the man who closed out the first Red Sox World Championship in eighty-six years, a pitcher making more than $7 million annually, admitted, "I'll never be channeled toward baseball. I'm not a baseball fan. I actually find baseball kind of boring. It's not my life. I can't sit around and watch nine innings of a baseball game."

My playing career was fun but unspectacular. Brother Bill was my first obstacle. When I was a kid, my big brother seemed to be better at baseball than just about anybody who ever played in Groton. They put him on the high school varsity as a starting rightfielder when he was in the *seventh grade.* By the time he was a sophomore, he was hitting home runs and winning a league championship as a pitcher. Bill is six years older than I am, and I'm convinced that I learned to report on sports by going to his games, then coming home and telling my parents and sisters what had happened.

Going to Fenway was not common. It was a once-a-year event, like Christmas and my birthday, and usually timed to soften the blow of my annual visit to the Lahey Clinic, where I was treated for asthma. Groton is only forty miles from Boston, but we didn't make many long drives when I was a kid, and a trip to the Hub was treated like a trip to Europe. We usually had to stop at the Howard Johnson's in Concord to mark the midpoint of our long journey. This made faraway Fenway even more fascinating. Thinking back, I remember a couple of times when my annual game was rained out, and to this day I deal poorly with unexpected disappointment. It reminds me of a rainout for that summer day I looked forward to the most.

Want more childhood trauma? Try this: I was *traded* in Little League. In the fourth grade I started out as a member of the Dodgers, but Groton's in-town Little League Dodgers and Yankees were too strong and the Giants and Braves too weak, so they put my name into a lottery for a dispersal draft to break up the superpowers. Probably because my brother was so good, the Braves assumed I would be good and took me for their roster. Sort of the Dominic DiMaggio effect. My Dodger coach, Andre Van Hoogen, called me before school one morning to break the news. I was crushed.

I loved Mr. Van Hoogen. He was the father of a raft of talented sons and daughters, and he'd come to our town from Chicago, where he'd coached Bryant and Greg Gumbel. Mr. Van Hoogen had had a childhood bout with polio that rendered his right arm useless. Still, he managed to hit us fungoes with his good arm—smoking a cigarette at the same time. It was impressive. He also was some kind of engineering genius and used a lot of big words. When we started calling a familiar umpire by his nickname, "Jake," Mr. Van Hoogen told us to knock it off. Said it sounded like we were in "cahoots" with Jake. *Cahoots.* I had to look that one up. Mr. Van Hoogen had a Fort Devens sticker on his car, which meant he could drive onto the army base in nearby Ayer and shop at the PX, where everything cost less. There were a lot of great men like Mr. Van Hoogen when I was a kid—men who'd served in World War II and come home never to speak of it again. Mr. Kopec, dad of my Little League teammate Woody, had fought on the beach in Normandy.

Then there was Mr. Zeamer, whose house was on Old Ayer Road. My friends and I knew it as the hallowed home of the great-looking Zeamer girls. My sister Ann was friendly with the bubbly Jackie Zeamer, and when my dad and I went to pick up Ann after a slumber party, Dad mentioned that Mr. Zeamer had been awarded the Congressional Medal of Honor for his bravery in World War II. None of the Zeamer girls ever mentioned this, and neither did their dad.

Tom Brokaw would later call them "the Greatest Generation," but we just knew these remarkable men as solid citizens who seemed to love the pace and beauty of small-town life. When I started behind the counter at the ice cream joint, the owner, Norm Johnson, told me the most important thing was serving customers quickly. He reminded me many of his customers had waited in lines during their hitch in the service, and they didn't ever want to wait in line again.

No doubt there are psychologists who'd enjoy getting inside the head of a little boy who was traded in Little League then grew up to be a wisecracking sports columnist, but we will have none of that here. Getting traded turned out to be okay, because I got two hats and a small trophy when the Dodgers won it all that year. I guess it was my World Series share for spending a portion of the season with the champs.

The real highlight of my baseball playing career came when I was 12 and led the league in home runs, hitting six in nine games. That first homer was the best. If you love playing baseball, hitting your first home run over a fence is easily a bigger deal than your first day of school, first kiss, first day on the job, or any of that other stuff. My first homer came on my first swing of the 1966 season off Yankee righty, Buzzy Lanni. Big Buzz threw hard and straight and I got him with the thirty-inch Al Kaline Louisville Slugger I'd purchased from Moisen's Hardware (later owned by the battery-bartering Sargent brothers) for six bucks. It was a beautiful, tapered, light bat with wide grain and perfect polish—like those shiny wooden checkerboards on the shelves of the souvenir shops at Hampton Beach. It even smelled good. It was my Wonderboy.

Standing on the mound on that perfect May Sunday, big Buzz held a right-out-of-the-box baseball that was as white as a Chiclet. That's how you knew the game was for real. In all forms of practice or backyard baseball, we'd use scuffed balls, taped balls, tennis balls, rubber balls, pimple balls, half-balls, anything. Not this time. Not on opening day. Hitting this ball would be like making the first sled marks on a hill of fresh snow. My heart beat fast as I stepped into the righthanded batter's box. This never changed. There was always an element of fright and anticipation whenever I went up to hit. Now I get that feeling when Sam is hitting. I suspect it's the same for all ballplayers and all parents.

Old Buzz's first pitch was a knee-high fastball, right where I like 'em. I did not put anything extra into the swing. I simply did what I'd done before thousands of times in my backyard. I followed the flight of the pitch, opened my hips, swung at the ball, and heard a *click*. The great Yaz once talked about that perfect hitter's moment when you take a big swing, connect with the sweet spot of the baseball, and feel absolutely nothing as your bat whooshes through the hitting zone. The hardball takes off like a Titleist struck by a two-iron. I experienced this only once.

There were no over-the-fence homers for me after that final Little League season. I was a scrawny second baseman/outfielder with little power. I played three years of varsity baseball at Groton High, but our teams were terrible and I was lucky to hit .250. We had more fun in the summertime, playing Babe Ruth games and commuting to surrounding towns in the flatbed of

Mr. Friedrich's green truck. He would carry the whole team, ten to twelve guys, in the back of the rusty old Chevy. His son, Albane, painted a "chartered" sign and taped it across the front of the truck. We would rumble across the bumpy, winding roads of Ayer, Pepperell, Shirley, and Lancaster, drinking Coca Cola from those 6½-ounce green bottles and singing songs we'd heard on *F Troop*. Then we would harass the other team's players ("This kid's got nothing! He's throwing junk!"), bash our way to victory, hop on the flatbed, and chug back to Groton. We might even stop for ice cream if old man Friedrich had a spare ten dollars. None of it would work today. You couldn't put kids in the back of a truck and you certainly could not hurl insults at the other team. Not now. Parents and officials would get in the way of the fun.

When I first touched down on Holy Cross's campus in September 1971, I went out for fall baseball for about a week. Once a national power, winning the NCAA Championship at Omaha in 1952, Holy Cross's baseball program was struggling by the time I arrived. I had brought my spikes and glove to school and went to a few captain's practices. I remember doing pretty well in batting practice at Fitton Field and getting the attention of the senior captain who was running the workout. But I knew the time demand would be large and the reward small. A plodding, .250 hitter from the Wachusett League wasn't good enough for Division I college baseball.

This was the proverbial fork in the road. In high school I had been class president, played three sports, worked twenty-five hours a week, wrote for the town newspaper, and even served as an audio-visual aide (the ultimate in dorkdom). I had promised myself to commit to only one extracurricular activity in college. It would not be baseball. I would write for the weekly student newspaper.

My first assignment for the vaunted *Crusader* was covering

the freshman football team. In my first story, I wrote that the freshman football team was in a "rebuilding year." And I wasn't even kidding.

Sports writing worked out pretty well in college. I was sports editor four weeks into sophomore year and soon realized that it would be prudent to spend more time on the school paper than on my studies. I nagged the *Boston Globe* editors and writers constantly for work, and after my junior year the *Globe* sports editor Dave Smith asked me if I would like to cover the Boston Neighborhood Basketball League during the summer. I would have walked on my lips through busted glass for any opportunity to get bylines in the *Globe*. It was then the paper of Peter Gammons (also a Grotonian), Ray Fitzgerald, Leigh Montville, Bud Collins, Will McDonough, Fran Rosa, and Bob Ryan. A tour through the *Globe* sports department was a walk through the clouds, and I spent the next three summers driving *Globe* cars in and out of sixteen different Boston neighborhoods, watching teenagers play summer basketball outdoors. It was the best training I could have had. I learned the city from Savin Hill to Mattapan, from Charlestown to Brighton. Due to forced school busing, the Hub was immersed in racial tension during those years, but my game knew no colors and no political points of view. I was a sportswriter for the *Boston Globe*. I covered and befriended men named Kevin Mackey, Leo Papile, and Jim Calhoun, guys who made it big in later years. But in those years, we were all just part of the Hub's hoop culture, sweating nightly and wondering when the city would ever cool down.

I graduated from college in 1975 and spent the next two years blissfully enjoying independence and learning the life of a sportswriter. I got to run quotes for the Associated Press at Fenway Park during the World Series season of 1975. It paid only seven dollars per night, but we could eat and drink all we wanted in the expansive, wood-paneled press dining room at Fenway. I introduced myself to old Mr. Tom Yawkey. I ate scrod and drank Scotch with Jumpin' Joe Dugin, who played third base for the 1927 Yankees. Jumpin' Joe had roomed with Babe Ruth and loved to tell stories about the Bambino. He would sometimes put his glass down, glance at me stuffing my face, and exclaim, "This kid eats more than Ruth!" I loved that.

Sitting in the smoky pressroom, I could listen to Billy Martin, Earl Weaver, Gene Mauch, Dick Williams, Bill Veeck, Calvin Griffith, Clark Booth, and all the writers I grew up reading. The stories got better as the night lengthened and the whiskey flowed. I quickly realized you learn the most by just listening.

This experience helped me land a job as a baseball writer at the *Baltimore Evening Sun* in the summer of 1977. I was 23 years old and vividly remember my first road trip to Cleveland. I found myself alone in an elevator with Brooks Robinson; he asked me my name and how old I was and said, "You're going to have a great time."

Brooks Robinson. How many times had I pretended I was him while tossing the rubber ball against the backdoor porch in Groton? Now, I was standing with him in an elevator at the Hollendon House in an American League city. I was in the big leagues, even if it was only as a small writer. The Orioles were then managed by Weaver and had a pitcher named Jim Palmer and a rookie designated hitter named Eddie Murray. All would make it to the Hall of Fame, as would a Maryland high school kid the O's drafted in 1978 — Cal Ripken Jr. Cal's dad, a third base coach, used to take me to dinner almost nightly at the old Dupont Plaza Hotel when the Orioles trained in Miami. When young Cal came to spring camp, the three of us would dine together.

The Orioles made it to the World Series two years after I left Boston. By then I was covering the Baltimore team for the *Washington Star*. A month before the '79 World Series, the O's made their final trip to Boston, and I hosted a Saturday night party in my high-rise corner room at the Boston Sheraton. Weaver and several of his coaches appeared, and the old men were quite taken with some of our young female friends. We still talk about Earl dancing in my room with several of the lovely Brissette sisters. The next day, I gave the maid ten dollars to clean up the room before my folks arrived for Sunday brunch. Proud of my expense account, I bought lunch for the folks, and I know Dad loved that. Later that day, before the game ended, I went to see my parents in section 27 of Fenway Park. It would be the last time I saw my dad.

The scheduled first game of the 1979 World Series in Baltimore was rained out. It snowed lightly overnight, and I stopped by old Memorial Stadium the next morning to see if Commissioner Bowie Kuhn might postpone game one for a second day. This was long before the cell phone era and I had no way of knowing that my family in Massachusetts was trying to reach me. When I walked into the Orioles' offices, a secretary said, "There he is," and whisked me into the office of veteran public relations director Bob Brown.

"It's about your dad," he said, stumbling to find words.

"He died, right?" I asked.

"Yes, he died," said Bob Brown.

It was a conversation I'd been expecting to have since my earliest days. Dad had had a lot of heart trouble as a young man and we were actually surprised he made it to the age of 64. I called my mom, brother, and sisters from Memorial Stadium, then flew home to Boston. We buried Dad three days later, and I rejoined the World Series in Pittsburgh before game four.

So it was always baseball. The last time I saw my dad was in Fenway Park. I was in Memorial Stadium when I learned he died. And he's buried in a small cemetery in East Pepperell, Massachusetts, right next to a Little League ball field.

I even met Marilou—who knows next to nothing about baseball—through baseball. It was six months after my father had passed and I was in Chicago with the Orioles, knocking back a few with Weaver and a radio guy in the Lion Bar at the Westin Hotel on Michigan Ave. A young woman—the only young woman at the Westin that night—kept running in and out of the bar (I found out later she was calling her boyfriend from the lobby payphone). I stopped her, offered to buy a drink, and pointed out that the great Earl Weaver was seated on a nearby stool. Naturally, she'd never heard of Earl. A month later, she would join me in Milwaukee when the Orioles were in town to play the Brewers. When I introduced her to Earl in the Pfister Hotel coffee shop at breakfast, he blurted, "In my day, we ordered room service!"

That Earl always was a sweet talker.

It mattered not that Marilou knew nothing about baseball. I got enough of it every day from fans and friends. John F. Kennedy was said to be relieved that Jackie never greeted him at the door with "What's new in Laos?" Marilou and I were married in February 1982 in Detroit (big draw, Detroit in February), and by then I was working at the *Boston Globe*, occasionally covering the Red Sox.

Baseball bookmarked our new family events. Sarah, who would grow up to become a catcher, was born in 1984, which was a good year to fly our family to Detroit because the Tigers were on their way to winning the World Series. When Kate was born in July 1985, I walked from Beth Israel Hospital to Fenway Park, where I handed out cigars behind the batting cage. Kate, who would become an outfielder, fell in love with baseball before any of our other kids, and when she was diagnosed with leukemia at the age of 8, it was the Jimmy Fund—the official charity of the Boston Red Sox—that saved her life. Sam was born on a Friday afternoon in October 1987, the day I was supposed to be flying to Detroit for a season-ending series between the Tigers and Blue Jays. The next day he (sort of) watched his first game, an extra-inning pitcher's duel between Jack Morris and Mike Flanagan. We brought Sam home on Sunday and I flew to Minnesota for the American League Championship Series the next day.

Baseball has been there at every important moment of my life. It has been very very good to me.

Sam

SARAH AND KATE SHAUGHNESSY inherited a well-documented family curse (on their dad's side) and needed braces to straighten their teeth. The process was long, uncomfortable, and expensive. When their younger brother reached the age of orthodontics, it was determined that he would not require braces. Only 11 years old, Sam had one reaction to his good fortune: he asked his parents for the cash difference. In Sam's mind, he was saving us money that we'd spent on his sisters, and he thought he should be compensated.

His name is Samuel William Shaughnessy, which sounds like maybe he was named after Theodore Samuel (Ted) Williams, but it's just coincidence. We had decided on "Sam" if it was a boy and William was my dad's name. It all seemed to fit when Sam first picked up a bat and swung from the left side and later dedicated his young life to baseball, baseball bats, and the science of hitting.

Sam had blond angelic hair when he was small, which sometimes drew odd glances from strangers who saw him with his mother. Marilou is half Sicilian and Sam inherited none of her Mediterranean features. He has green eyes and a crooked sly smile and his hair, unfortunately, has taken on the coarseness and color of his dad's. (Like me, he can also go a week without shaving before anyone says anything.) When Sam gets a buzz cut, he's reminded that he looks a little like Red Sox outfielder Trot Nixon. That's just fine with Sam. They both hit lefthanded and work from a dramatically spread stance.

One thing Sam got from his mother's gene pool is the upper torso of a Teamster. Marilou's dad is 100 percent Polish with wide shoulders, thick arms, and meaty hands. As Sam's baseball skills blossomed through high school, his arms and chest expanded, giving him the look of a young man who maybe had swallowed a couple of barbells. While most of the best players in our region grew to be six foot two with rangy, limber bodies (the kind the pro scouts love), Sam grew sideways. It's pretty clear that he's never going to be six feet tall, but I remind him that he's just a little thicker than Bill Mueller (five foot ten, 180 lbs.), who won a batting title with the Red Sox in 2003.

Sam's first birthday party was held at our new/old home in the Hunnewell Hill section of Newton, Massachusetts. Newton is a suburb of Boston with over 80,000 citizens, most of whom at one time or another seem to have written books, seen therapists, and driven Volvos. Newton leads the nation in psychologists and bleeding hearts. The median income for a Newton family exceeds $100,000, and three times since 1999 it has been named the safest city in America. Recess at Sam's old elementary school features a "tug of peace" because the old-fashioned tug of war is too aggressive and offensive for some of our overthinking, baby boomer parents. Birth announcements in our local paper come under the heading of "arrivals" because we don't want to offend parents who've adopted children. When corporate honchos attempted to open a Dunkin' Donuts franchise at the busy corner near our home, neighbors galvanized and protested with the fever you'd expect if somebody had threatened to open a sex toy shop.

I love our house. As I type these words, I'm sitting in my

office at the back of the second floor, and I can hear Sam coming in the front door and running up the steps to his bedroom on the front side of the house. I hear the clacking of the wood baseball bats in his bag. It's early in the school year and Sam's just come in from an afternoon of hitting.

A large portion of the wall of my office is covered by a mural I assembled when I was in high school. It's a collage of color sports photographs clipped from the pages of *Sport* magazine and *Sports Illustrated*, circa 1965 to 1970. Bill Russell, Johnny Unitas, Ray Nitschke, and Hank Aaron have been watching my fingers fly across the keyboard for parts of five decades. They are frozen in time, eternal heroes of my youth, the godfathers of the Tom Bradys, Manny Ramirezes, and Paul Pierces I write about today.

Our big old (1900) house has three floors, six bedrooms, three crummy old bathrooms, and a soon-to-be-finished basement, which always had a pool table and Ping-Pong when the kids were younger. We've got two washers, two dryers, two fridges, and lots of dust and cracked windows on every floor. Just about all the window sashes are broken. You can feel the wind coming through the creaky window casings when you stand close during winter storms. The house is big, cluttered, and drafty. Things are always breaking, but I love it more than any building I've known and that would include the house where I grew up in Groton, Massachusetts, and Fenway Park—my two other all-time favorite abodes. Houses have souls and this well-worn structure is full of grace, warmth, and lingering laughter. It's warm even when it's cold. It's safe even when we're watching world calamities on television. It was home to babysitters from Sweden when the kids were small, and it was home to dozens of international students who came to the States to learn English at a school in downtown Boston. It's been home to Alexis Mongo, Sam's Metco brother since kindergarten, a city kid who's had a bed and toothbrush here since he was five years old. It's been home to half of the Newton North basketball team during winter break (the hoopsters like to make pancakes when we're on Christmas holiday), and it's been home to several players on the Boston University softball team who needed a place to stay for the summer. It's been home to *Globe* summer interns, my daughter Kate's boyfriend, Marilou's parents, and all the aunts and uncles and cousins who've visited or lived with us for an entire summer. Sam and I once counted the bed and couch capacity and came up with the magic number of twenty-three. We exceeded that number a few times when Kate and Sarah had team sleepovers during high school volleyball, field hockey, and softball days.

There are no school buses trolling the Hunnewell Hill section of Newton. Our kids walk or ride bikes for the first nine years of their public education. Neighborhood watchdogs are legion. We still have block parties and pig roasts. We get weekly milk delivery in old-timey glass bottles. Tom the mailman is allowed to stroll into our home and help himself to cold water from the Poland Spring cooler in the kitchen. Nobody calls the cops if a neighbor has a loud party—better to crash said party. Growing up in Groton, I remember reading hilarious police reports about a "suspicious vehicle" in a neighborhood. That was code for "a car we could not immediately identify." Anything new or different was immediately suspicious. And all these years later it's the same in our Newton neighborhood. Woe to the suspicious vehicle. We joke that you can't walk around the Hill without a passport and Sam knows that if he's seen driving too fast on the way to school, we'll know about it by dinnertime—from multiple sources.

Kate was diagnosed with leukemia in 1993, when Sam was in kindergarten, and I'll never forget the way the neighborhood rallied. Stacked like cordwood, homemade lasagnas packed our basement freezer. Neighbors put a grocery list inside our door every few days. We'd check off the items we needed and bags of groceries would arrive later in the day.

"Just like in the old days," Marilou's mother would say after finding another pie or dinner feast cooling on the front porch.

While we spent all of our time with Kate at Children's Hospital, Sam and Sarah were invited on playdates and taken to Chuck E. Cheese. You don't forget that kind of unconditional love.

Our house was always full of sounds. Kids laughing. Kids arguing. Canned laughter as the girls watched yet another episode of *Friends*. Kate practicing the drums. Sam dribbling a basketball in his room, loosening the plaster on the ceiling over the TV room. When the kids got older, and there were cars and boyfriends and girlfriends, we embraced and encouraged the noise. When there was noise, we knew they were home. Only silence was troublesome. Silence meant one of two things: 1. The kids were not home and we had no idea what was really going on; or 2. They were home and it was too damn quiet for anyone to be up to any good. Pretty soon that silence is going to mean that the job of child-raising is done and they are gone for good.

One feature we lack is a big rolling lawn for ball games. The homes in our neighborhood are close together and nobody's got enough yard for a decent Wiffle ball or touch football game. Sam outgrew our quilt-size lawn by the time he was 8.

Little Sam always seemed to have a bat in his hands and he always batted left—a first in our family. I once asked Ted Williams why he batted left and if he'd ever tried hitting righthanded. Ted reacted as if I'd asked him to speak Portuguese. In Ted's world, there was only one way to hit. The best hitters were always lefty hitters. The baseball world is dominated by righty pitchers and we all know the lefthanded hitters' batter's box is significantly closer to first base. There would be no righthanded hitting for Theodore Samuel Williams. None for Samuel William Shaughnessy either.

Sam was forever looking for someone to pitch to him. In the summer of 1992, when Sam was 4, we rented a giant house in Pocasset, a beach town at the foot of the Cape Cod Canal. It was a group rental, shared with Marilou's coworkers, and while his sisters and cousins went to swim and sunbathe, Sam could always be seen standing around with his red, fat bat in his hand, looking for someone to toss Wiffle balls his way. Returning from my daily run one afternoon, I encountered tiny Sam, who wanted to know if I could throw him a few pitches. I told him I had to go inside to use the bathroom but would return for some batting practice. While I was in the first-floor stall, I heard one of our friends, Harry King, talking to Sam and it was pretty clear from the conversation that the little kid had convinced the man to play some ball. Harry was one of those cool grownups—single, fit, bookish, and owner of his own drum set. It occurred to me that he might underestimate Sam's hitting prowess, and I wondered if he might be standing a little too close when—still in the bathroom—I heard him saying, "Here you go, little guy, let's see if you can hit this."

"*Whomp!*"

"*Pow.*"

"Ouch."

I darted out of the bathroom and back to the front lawn, where Harry was sprawled on the grass, rubbing his temple and checking to see if his glasses were broken. Sam was standing nearby, holding his fat bat, laughing at the man on the ground.

"This kid can really hit," said Harry.

It's pretty much been like that ever since. Sam was slow to speak (two years of speech therapy when he was a toddler), reluctant to pick up a book (Ted always said he saved his eyes by not reading), hated to swim, was afraid of fireworks, and could not ski. He didn't have a very good arm, never developed an outside shot on the basketball court, and his football instincts were terrible. He couldn't run long distances. He could be stubborn and lazy, his room was a mess, and he mumbled all the time. He and his friends seemed to speak in code and I secretly wished for subtitles like the kind they use in foreign films at the West Newton Cinema. One of my friends correctly noted, "The only times I can understand Sam are when he's pissed off or he wants something."

This child was not a Renaissance man.

But he could hit.

Sam advanced through the normal channels of youth baseball, playing T-ball, then coach-pitch, then minors, then major league Little League. Sam was able to compete in the Little League "majors" when he was 10, and I always thought it was a good idea for him to "play up." Invented by families with two or more male children, the concept of "playing up" starts with a younger brother playing against older brothers. Veteran coaches will tell you that a player with a lot of older brothers is almost always better than another player of the same age who might be a first-born or an only child. You simply get better playing against older kids, and since Sam didn't have any older brothers, I knew he would benefit from playing with 12-year-olds when he was 10.

His White Sox Little League (minors) cap was the first to be hung on a nail on his bedroom wall, and twelve years later fifteen of those team hats hang side by side, symbolic of hardball progression. Those caps will be there as long as we stay in this old house. I have my sports photomural. Sam has his caps.

Sports connect generations. Parents and children don't go to rock concerts together. They are obligated to disagree about politics, religion, fashion, food, hair, and morality. But they still gather to watch the Red Sox in the family room, even when they can't find common ground anywhere else. I take Sam to Fenway and we strain our necks to look around the same poles that blocked the views of my father and grandfather. I go to Sam's games and remember what it is I loved about sports in the first place.

Sam always loved baseball more than the other games, and he loved hitting more than baseball. He loves hitting the way Ted loved hitting. Sam can watch hitting videos all day. He's never far from one of his bats. And his sisters still laugh when they remember watching him from a kitchen window, playing alone in a driveway when we were road-tripping in Montana, hitting rocks out of his hand and posing like Ken Griffey Jr. before going into his home run trot.

One of his earliest school essays was entitled "Hitting." He led off with "Hitting is my life. I cannot think of many things I would rather do than step up to the plate. I could take batting practice every day until my hands bleed and still love it. I love everything that has to do with hitting. I love bats, batting gloves, batting helmets, pine tar, doughnuts, fences, anything and everything that is associated with hitting. A baseball bat to me is a piece of art, a stick of wood crafted into a thing of beauty."

I missed his first Little League home run. Sam's Metco brother Alexis was there for the historic shot and retrieved the baseball from the small creek beyond the right field fence at Murphy Playground. A week later, I was sitting in the aluminum stands at the Murph and saw Sam hit a fly ball over the fence in right-center off a lanky lefty. It was quite a thrill to see my son rounding first after the second homer of his career. Then, before you could say Barry Bonds, I wanted to put a bag over my head. Sam was in a full-blown home run trot. He was stylin' his way around the bases. He was taunting the opposition.

This stuff didn't happen when I was a kid. If you were lucky enough to hit a home run, you circled the bases with dignity. When you crossed home plate, you shook hands with the on-deck hitter, who'd be standing on the other side of the dish with his hand extended. You looked like a couple of stockbrokers meeting for lunch. That's the way Mantle and Maris always did it. It had a certain understated style.

Now this. Hot-dogging from 11-year-olds. We know where it comes from. The beast is known as *ESPN SportsCenter* and it's where our precious games sadly morphed into moronic entertainment. Muhammad Ali is probably the one who got it all started and then we had Joe Namath and those white shoes and then basketball players who decided that style was more important than substance. There's no room for fundamentally sound, square-shooting Larry Bird anymore. It's all about whatever you can do to bring attention to yourself to get a top-ten highlight. I regard the end zone dance—take out a Sharpie and sign the ball, make a call on your cell phone, do a couple of pull-ups on the crossbar, or use the goal post to wipe your butt—as a crime against sportsmanship. Barry Sanders was one athlete who suggested dignity, telling young players to "act like you've been there before." But too many of our young players would rather look good and miss a shot than do something awkward and put the ball in the goal.

So there was my 11-year-old son, showing off. I said nothing until we got into the car, then offered, "Sam, nice home run. What didn't Dad like?"

"Showing off around the bases?" he asked.

"Right," I said.

About a week later, I was on assignment in Arizona, responsible for talking to Mark McGwire about the upcoming Home Run Derby at Fenway Park before the 1999 All Star game. This was in the days after McGwire set the country on fire, hitting seventy home runs in 1998. It was also in the days before the steroid scandal of 2005, when McGwire walked into a congressional hearing with feet of clay. In 1999, Big Mac was still a diamond god, particularly to a certain young home run hitter.

I interviewed McGwire about Fenway Park and the upcoming Home Run Derby, then told him about Sam and the home run trot and asked him for a little parental help. Sam was born the same weekend as McGwire's first son in 1987, and Mark was only too happy to speak into my tape recorder about home run decorum. Simple stuff: put your head down and run around the bases. Don't try to show up the pitcher. He's not trying to show you up.

Sam was in the bathtub when I came home from the trip. It was nighttime, but I couldn't wait. I went into the bathroom and set the recorder down on the corner of the tub.

"Here's what Mark McGwire says you do when you hit a home run," I said, pushing the Play button as I set down the small machine.

We never talked about it after that. Lucky boy. He got the message directly from the then-god of home runs.

Newton North's diamond, Murphy Field, is perfectly symmetrical, with a green wooden outfield fence and bleachers behind both dugouts and home plate. In our section of town, we allow signage on the outfield fences, and local hardware stores and landscaping companies support the league in exchange for ads on the fence. Other parts of our PC city ban signage at their ballparks and there was a big to-do one year when a local pub had a sign on its outfield wall. Concerned citizens worried that the league was promoting drinking, so all signs were banned. Meanwhile, I'm told that in parts of St. Louis, there are Anheuser-Busch beer stands in the middle of Little League complexes . . . for the dads and moms, of course.

I stayed out of Little League politics. Lesson one: *never, never, never* offer to umpire. Do I make myself clear? *Never.* You know why. If you make a call that favors your child's team, you will hear about it from some nitwit dad who has a player on the other team. If you rule against your own kid's team, you get the silent treatment from your own family. Also, no matter how well you think you know baseball, something will happen that you have never seen before and you will not know which call to make. I made the mistake of offering to render a decision in a girls' softball game when Kate was in middle school. We had an episode that would have highlighted *SportsCenter* if it had happened in the World Series. The play involved a simple ground ball to the pitcher and a simple throw to first base. The throw beat the runner, but it was a one-hopper that the first baseman somehow managed to secure between her knees. No kidding. Her glove was nowhere near the ball, but when it skipped in front of her, it bounced toward her kneecaps and she grasped the ball by closing her knees together.

Safe or out? You make the call.

I called the kid safe. But I wasn't sure. Somehow, even though the first baseman had control of the ball, it didn't look like a legal catch. After considerable debate, I inquired if anyone had a cell phone. I called the American League office and asked to speak with Marty Springstead, a former big league ump I'd known back in the days when I covered the Orioles and he was always throwing Earl Weaver out of games. Marty told me that the baserunner was safe. The fielder needs to have possession of the ball, and possession means the ball must be in the fielder's hand or glove. It's not like in the NFL, when a receiver would be credited with a catch even if he secured the ball by having it jammed into his facemask. Not in baseball. An outfielder who falls down and has a ball land on his stomach has not made a catch. He must secure the ball in his hand or glove.

On another day, when I watched another dad volunteer to umpire, I witnessed a hideous scene after a close play at home plate. The little girl pitcher had run in to cover home after a wild pitch, and she took the throw from the catcher as the baserunner steamed in from third. The dad/ump ruled "safe," which sent the pitcher into a Weaveresque tantrum. The little girl ultimately wound up on her back, crying and kicking her legs, not unlike *Animal House*'s John Belushi during Otis Day and the Knights' rendition of "Shout." Next thing you knew, the softball mom was kneeling over her daughter, saying, "It's okay, Lindsey. The umpire knows that he lied. He has to look at himself in the mirror knowing that. You'll be okay."

Then there was the perfect May night when a team from the West Newton Little League arrived at our ballpark and immediately turned back because their coach would not be part of any game involving the umpire who'd been assigned to work that night. I didn't want to get involved, but I simply couldn't believe this was happening. We had more than twenty kids and dozens of parents gathered on a beautiful night for baseball, but there was not going to be a game because the coach didn't like the umpire. He said the ump had been verbally abusive to his kids. He said he had warned league officials. As his little players walked back to their cars, I caught up with a few parents and asked them if they were okay with this. They nodded and agreed. They'd rather forfeit than play another game with this umpire.

Not me. Not now. Not ever. Let the kids play the game. The world is going to be full of teachers, coaches, and bosses that our kids do not like. What is the message when we tell them it's better to go home than to stick around and play the game?

My all-time favorite parent-as-jerk moment came when Sarah was coaching field hockey at Newton North and one of the dads from the other team refused to put out a cigar he'd lit while standing on the sideline. The guy thought the request to lose his stogie was one of our endless PC rules, when, in fact, it is state regulation that prohibits all smoking on school grounds. After much consultation with captains, coaches, and officials (I think he made one of our players cry), the man stormed off the premises, and the Newton team was awarded a corner opportunity. Proving that there is a sports god, our girls scored their only goal on the corner and the visiting team went home with a 1–1 tie, knowing that one dad's cigar had cost them a win. The non-victory cigar. The anti–Red Auerbach. Hang down your head, Dad.

For anyone who loves to play baseball, there is almost nothing better than your last year of Little League. It's when you are 12 and finally big enough to master the small diamond. It's when you can hit the ball over the fence and give pointers to the younger kids. It's when you are almost ready for the next level.

The inimitable Jerry Sack came into Sam's life when he was a 12-year-old Little Leaguer. Jerry is a legitimate Newton legend, a Little League bird dog, annually scouting all five Newton leagues and assembling a traveling all-star team of 12-year-olds. Crusty, crude (did he really moon the crowd back in the day?), and well past middle age, he could have played the Walter Matthau role in the original *Bad News Bears*. He drives a giant black Caddy and deals in precious metals. Jerry, who is Jewish, loves to recruit the hardscrabble Italian kids from the Lake section of town (where there is no water), and he once told me, "When in doubt, always draft the kid whose name ends in a vowel—unless it's Shapiro!"

Stocked with big, strong kids who could hit the ball over the fence, Jerry's team went to tournaments throughout Massachusetts. They wore ultra-cheap, powder-blue hats and shirts and won most of their games. Sam struggled at the start. He wasn't sure he belonged, but he fought his way through and finished batting in the three hole and reaching base in fifteen of his final sixteen Little League at-bats.

There's beauty in comfort when you play sports and somehow outgrow the dimensions of the game. It happens to young ballplayers just before they reach the next level, and it happens to a few professional athletes who reach a point where they are men in a game against boys. Wilt Chamberlain must have felt like this when he averaged fifty points a game. Michael Jordan, too. Watching Barry Bonds early in the twenty-first century gave one the same feeling, but then, of course, it turned out Barry was cheating.

I felt this only once: Eric Monroe's barn on Blossom Lane in Groton, Massachusetts. It was the mid-1960s, and we hung baskets inside at both ends of the big cold barn at the top of Mr. Monroe's driveway. I was older and bigger than most of the boys who were playing in our pickup games in those days, and I was never on the losing side. I learned how to make shots over the rafter in the middle of our makeshift court. It was a feeling of absolute invulnerability. There was never a doubt. There was no way I could lose. I was only 12, but I had no challenge, nothing to shake my confidence. Years later, sitting courtside at the Boston Garden, I would watch Larry Joe Bird impose his will on basketball games and win just about every time. He could do whatever he wanted. He would go to the foul line in the final two minutes and everyone knew he'd make the shot. And in my own odd way, I could relate to what he was feeling. It was the feeling I had in the barn all those years ago—only Larry was doing it against the world's best players. Absolute invulnerability.

After Little League, Babe Ruth baseball was next for Sam. It's an interesting leap. Boys go from 12 to 13, the mound goes from 45 feet to 60 feet, the base paths go from 60 to 90, and the fences from 200 to 340. It's like landing in Paris and trying to understand the locals after taking one year of high school French.

By the time Sam was a freshman in high school, he'd established himself as a pretty fair local hitter. I figured he was a cinch to leapfrog the freshman team and land on the junior varsity. Still, there was a minor incentive to playing for the Newton North freshman because Kent Damon, Matt Damon's dad, coached the team. A graying, handsome man in his early fifties,

Kent coached the freshman for the fun of it. Legend held that his famous son would stop by for at least one practice per year, and the kids loved to hear stories about Matt's ballplaying as a youngster in Cambridge. While working on a magazine profile, I spent a day with Matt in 2004 and noted that he was most animated when his limo drove past a Cambridge Little League field where he'd hit a home run when he was 12. Better than the Oscar probably.

Kate was a senior softball captain when Sam was a freshman, and she got word that Sam was tearing it up at the high school baseball tryouts. Veteran coaches considered him the best hitter in the school but didn't want to rush him onto varsity where he might struggle, so they put him on the junior varsity team. He hit .500 in half a season with the junior varsity before getting called up.

It was a heady time for a 15-year-old boy. He'd gone to Legion tryouts just a few days earlier and made the team when he launched a homer over the rightfield fence that shattered the windshield of Post 440's star pitcher. He was also experiencing some lower back pain, and I'd received a rather alarming phone call from his doctor on the same day Sam was called up to the high school varsity. There was something on Sam's back x-ray that concerned the doctors. It was either a skeletal abnormality that had been there since birth . . . or it was a tumor. They wanted him to have a CAT scan and an MRI.

I dissolved. It was too reminiscent of what had happened to Kate. We'd learned she had leukemia only because we'd taken her to the clinic when she complained of back pain. Now, here was Sam, readying for his first varsity game, as a freshman no less, and the possibility existed that this might be his last game. I knew I was overreacting, but I just had a bad feeling. When I found the field at Milton, the Newton varsity coach, Joe Siciliano, proudly showed me his new lineup card. He had Sam batting cleanup.

Ouch. I told the coach that Sam would miss school tomorrow because of medical tests. And then I watched Sam go 1-4 in his first varsity game. He looked small and overmatched. His hit was an infield hit.

We went to Children's Hospital at eight the next morning, and I never told Sam the potential seriousness of the situation. By noon, the doctor was telling me that everything was normal. Sam played a home game against Brookline the next day and struck out four times. Truly overmatched. He cared deeply. Too much. And that's why he wasn't able to hit. I cared not a bit, not anymore. He did not have a tumor. There would be plenty of time to get out of this slump.

Knowing that Sam was worried about his nonhitting, the way I'd been worried about the nontumor, I gave him a copy of Willie Mays's autobiography and opened it up to the section on Willie's first month in the big leagues in 1951. Mays went 1-25 when he first got to the majors and told his manager, Leo Durocher, "I can't hit up here." Durocher said that as long as he was manager of the Giants, Mays would be his centerfielder. Mays wound up hitting .264 with 20 homers in 121 games and went on to be perhaps the greatest baseball player who ever lived.

As the high school season drew to a close (the North varsity was stumbling through a lifeless season, well below .500), Newton North Athletic Director T. J. Williams selected Sam to speak to a packed house of eighth graders and parents regarding the leap from junior high school sports to high school sports. Marilou and I were stunned. Sam? Speaking to an auditorium of people? Without subtitles?

"He'll do great," said the veteran AD. "He played three sports and we like to pick someone out who can use a little push in this area. You watch. He'll surprise you."

Sam was still in his baseball uniform, spreading infield dust on the stage as he shuffled to the podium. His clay-stained uniform jersey (number 24 in honor of Ken Griffey Jr. and Manny Ramirez) was unbuttoned and he had dirt smudges on his face as he slouched slightly behind the microphone. He looked like a ballplayer. He had scribbled notes, but he talked to the audience without reading. He told the kids and their parents that sports had been a great way for him to get involved in the big high school. He said that playing three sports had forced him to be organized about his studies. His speech was peppered with "like"s and "you know"s, but he pulled it off, and I thought about what T. J. had said. More often than not, veteran teachers and school administrators know what they are talking about. They've seen thousands of students pass through their corridors and they know kids.

Sam didn't get many varsity hits, but you could see he was feeling more comfortable at the end of the season. He went directly into the Legion season, where some of the boys were already playing in college. They all had cars. Too proud to ride his bike, Sam got dropped off by his parents a safe distance from where all the players were gathered.

The Newton Legion coach is Manny Connerney, who looks like former Tiger Hall of Fame skipper Sparky Anderson and sometimes sounds like Earl Weaver. Manny was one of the finest athletes in the history of our town, a high school running back with bullet speed and a Ty Cobb clone on the baseball diamond. He's a retired fireman, half Irish, half Italian. When he's not watching sports, coaching, or spending time with his family, he's tending to the carrier pigeons he keeps in a large gray shed next to his home in the Lake section of town. In the dugout, as in all other matters of work and play, Manny is decidedly old school. He's a my-way-or-the-highway kind of guy. I have never heard him second-guess himself. This streak of stubbornness can be an asset for any coach. When Manny's head hits the pillow at night, he's not wondering if he made the right move earlier in the day.

Salty language and diminutive stature aren't the only things he has in common with the likes of Sparky and Earl. Manny doesn't hold grudges, at least not against his players. He'll scream at a kid in the second inning then give him a pat on the back in the bottom of the third. That's how it was when I covered Earl for five years in Baltimore and Washington. He'd chew out your ass for something you wrote but offer you a beer before you left his office. He did not want to end things badly. It was the same with his ballplayers, who were sometimes united in their hatred of Earl, but it helped get him into the Hall of Fame.

Happily for Sam, Manny took one look at Sam in the cage and decided that Sam was a hitter. Nothing would ever change that. There's a lot of this in sports evaluation. Most coaches and scouts are guilty. They get a first impression of a player and stick with it, regardless of subsequent performance or failures. It has something to do with pride in one's own ability to evaluate talent. It has been the undoing of hundreds of scouts and coaches through the years.

Manny's confidence in his own evaluation didn't flag when Sam struck out four times in one varsity game. When the Legion's summer season started, Manny put Sam into the seventh spot in his batting order, and—Durocher-like—he never took him out.

Safe at the bottom of the order, surrounded in the lineup by bigger, older, more imposing hitters, Sam got a steady diet of fastballs down the middle. He didn't get any hits in his first game, and I figured he was bound for the bench . . . but not with Manny in charge. In his fourth game, Sam legged out an infield chopper for his first Legion hit. Any hitter will tell you, sometimes that's all it takes. Next time up, Sam crushed a long triple to right-center.

After that, he didn't slow down until his Legion team reached the state tournament in Worcester. Starting with the infield hit, he had nine consecutive hits. He finished with 28 hits in 60 at-bats (.467). He went to a college showcase at Bentley and hit a home run and a triple. He took fifteen swings against a pitching machine at Fenway, part of a Jimmy Fund promotion, and hit a ball eight rows over the visitors' bullpen. He developed a keen sense of the strike zone and would not go after bad pitches. He was almost too selective. He could pull the ball and hit it the other way. He was faster than he looked. A couple of college coaches told me he had "recruitable" bat speed.

Downer dad that I am, I've always been there to remind Sam how many great hitters there are in places like Florida, Texas, and California. Not to mention the Dominican Republic. Too many parents get caught up in the dream of college scholarships and professional contracts. I know better. There are hundreds, *thousands* of 18-year-old baseball players with better skills than my son. I see them every year at spring training in Fort Myers: the kids who dominate their high school leagues, sign professional contracts, get the write-up in the local paper, receive the shaving kit from their parents, and shove off to jerkwater minor league towns where they struggle to hit .200 against 6-6 lefthanders who throw 95 miles an hour but can't hit a billboard from twenty feet. And that's why the message for Sam has been to have a Plan B. It's okay to dream about playing professional baseball, but the strategy is to see if baseball will help him get the education he needs to get a fair start in the professional world.

Sam attended several college and professional showcases in the summer before eleventh grade and was suddenly mindful of his competition for college baseball slots. He converted from first base to outfield, where his relatively weak arm and poor instincts were exposed. Most of the kids at the showcases threw better and went back on the ball with more confidence. A few of them even hit the ball harder and farther, a humbling but necessary education for my baseball-centric son.

"Dad, some of these guys are really good!" Sam observed.

It was with this newfound perspective that Sam went into his junior year of baseball, and it was clear from the start that he was putting too much pressure on himself. Every at-bat became a make-or-break experience. He'd set ridiculous goals for himself and feared that every at-bat would determine his entire future. He started off the season 0-8 and was something like 2-15 when he went to Walpole and had a chance to play in front of the former Red Sox manager Joe Morgan and a scout from the Dodgers. It was painful. Sam went 0-5, striking out three times, and after the game looked at me and asked, "Why can't I hit?"

Tough question. I told him what I always told him at times like that, a string of clichés that spilled out of me as if they were coming from a tired old sportswriter hack: *Relax. You'll always be able to hit. The best hitters fail seven out of ten times. Remember what Tom Hanks said in* A League of Their Own: *"It's supposed to be hard. If it was easy, everybody'd do it." And finally, try to go back to your earliest days of baseball and remember what it is you love about it.*

He wrote about this internal battle, the bane of all athletic performance, in the spring semester of that same year. The school essay served nicely as his college application writing sample a few months later when he formally applied to Boston College. Entitled "Life Is a Silly Game," it read:

My life is a silly game. The game I play is in my mind. For the most part, I play against myself. This is not a game like Chutes and Ladders or musical chairs. The game I play is a puzzle, like a challenge. I have worried that I might be legally insane. I over-analyze everything. And not just in a comical Seinfeld way either—in all aspects of life. I see everything ten steps ahead. I drive myself nuts.

My biggest challenge is not to think myself to death. If I get a 78 on a math test, I instantly think: I want to get a 90 for the term for an A-, a 7.7 towards the grade point average at Newton North High School—there will be four tests this term—I need 360 points out of 400—360 minus 78 equals 282—divided by three equals 94—and that is what I must average for the next three tests. Another example; baseball. I know what my average will be if I go 0-4, 1-3, 2-5, 3-4, and so on. How does all this over-analyzing hurt me? It crushes my confidence.

On any given day I could go from thinking that I am not going to be able to get into Dunkin' Donuts University all the way to thinking I am a shoo-in for Harvard. I do not understand why this happens, but I cannot seem to do anything about it. I struggle to stay consistent and not get too down. Now there is the game connection. Mind game. My mind's a game.

I love baseball. But it might kill me. If I go 0-4, I want to hang myself in the closet; conversely, if I go 3-4 with a home run, I want the Red Sox to select me as their first draft pick. I love to play, I just hate when I suck. It is harder for me to stop myself from bashing my helmet against the wall after striking out than it is for me to hit an 88-mile-per-hour fastball. The challenge in my life is all mental. The mind game I play over and over. When something goes wrong, preventing myself from thinking my life is over is the only way for me to win.

Fortunately, Sam knows nothing of the mind games that are played in the third base bleachers and beyond the chain link fence in right. Watching can be more nerve-racking than playing. The kids get to use their bodies to release tension and aggression. Parents just sit in the stands and die a little every time they see their kid fail. Detroit Tiger manager Jim Leyland said that watching his teen son play baseball was far more stressful than managing against the St. Louis Cardinals in the 2006 World Series. I cannot imagine what it must be like to have a son who is saddled with the responsibility of pitching. It's awful and can be awkward. What do you say to make the pitcher's dad feel better when he just walked home the winning run? Like Sam, my life is a silly game when I'm watching him hit. Superstitions abound. If he gets a hit his first time up, I'll be sitting in the same spot, holding my hands in the same place next time he bats. If he strikes out in the first, you'll see me standing someplace else when he comes up again in the third. And woe to the well-meaning stranger who tries to ask me something about the Red Sox when my son is hitting. The kid only bats four or five times a game. A little quiet. *Please.*

Sam came out of his April slump in grand fashion, and by the end of the year he was back where he wanted to be with his name in the *Globe* among the statistical leaders and four homers and a steal of home to beat Brookline. He was good enough to make the All Scholastic page in the *Boston Herald*, though not quite good enough to get the same recognition in my own paper. Ever mature, I posted Sam's *Herald* photo and the accompanying article on the wall of my cubicle at the *Globe*.

Then came the State Tournament and the best day of Sam's life. He hit three home runs in a first-round upset victory over Malden Catholic.

It was surreal. We might not yet believe it if not for home video captured by Kate: a laser over the fence in right-center, a high fly to center—carried over the wall by wind and metal— then a well-crushed ball over the fence in left-center. After he was intentionally walked in the eighth, Jarred Amato, a dedicated senior, the hardest-working player on the team, delivered a game-winning, bases-loaded double. Several hundred fans attended, including a Boston College coach, and Red Sox scout Jeremy Kapstein. Best of all for Sam, his uncle Bill was visiting from Arizona, watching him play for the first time since Little League.

"Unbelievable," Bill told Sam, "Three homers in a game. I think I only did that twice."

Sam got a kick out of that.

Already connected by bloodlines and life in the batter's box, Sam and his stockbroker uncle have been a club of two since that day. Sam calls his uncle Bill's 800-number with instructions to buy or sell, and then they talk about hitting.

Life changed for Sam after that magical afternoon at Newton North. Letters from colleges started coming to the house nearly every day, and it was clear that the coaches at Boston College were taking him more seriously. His exploits were covered in the newspaper and briefly became a topic for the local sports radio station. One of the commentators mentioned the fact that Dan Shaughnessy's son hit three home runs in a high school tournament game. The cohost said, "Wouldn't it be great if the kid made it to the big leagues and then fell flat on his face?"

I warned Sam about this. My job gave him rare exposure to big league baseball and major league ballplayers. He'd seen the stars up close and had conversations with a few. He'd had a chance to hit at the Sox minor league complex and got some instruction from the Sox's hitting coach, Ron Jackson. But the downside was that he would sometimes be a marked man. He'd have to demonstrate uncommon restraint, and he'd probably have to be a little better and tougher than the next guy in order to avoid the appearance that he was being favored because of his dad.

About a month after the high school season ended, Sam got a letter from a Red Sox scout inviting him to a professional showcase in Wilmington, North Carolina. He would be one of three Massachusetts boys on a team of players from the northeast in a tournament involving five other major league clubs and a couple hundred of the top high school players on the East Coast.

He'd done a bunch of college showcases, including a week at Stanford where he received a woeful evaluation ("average high school ability, not draftable, junior college ability in future"). This was different. The pro showcase cost virtually nothing and was attended by serious college and pro scouts. Most important, it was by invitation only. This was not something you could buy for your kid, and they weren't interested in who Sam's dad was. The competition would be far more difficult than anything Sam had experienced.

Naturally, the opportunity also presented us with one of the greatest scheduling conflicts in family history. I'm still bitter about missing a 1967 Pony League playoff game because I had to serve as an altar boy at my sister Mary's wedding. Since that day, I have always been an advocate for team over family—unless it's a funeral or an emergency involving a parent or sibling. Marilou feels quite differently, and through the years there've been a few tempests over family trips not taken in the name of sports.

As soon as I saw the dates of Sam's potential big trip to North Carolina, I knew there'd be a bad moon risin' over the House of Shaughnessy. The pro showcase was scheduled for the same dates we had already booked for a family reunion trip. And not just any trip. Marilou's parents, nearing 80, were taking all of their children and grandchildren—a tidy gang of twenty-three—to Sicily for a week. This junket had been in the works for over a year and fell under the category of command performance. No weekend passes. All furlough canceled. It was shaping up as Dan Shaughnessy and the cast of *The Godfather* for seven sweaty days in Palermo, and it was not to be missed. All of us were looking forward to it and the plane tickets had already been purchased.

Still, in my mind, Sam had to skip the family trip. For him, this tryout could be a life-changing experience. He was almost ready to turn 18 and had decided that baseball was his ticket to college admission. It was the thing he cared about more than cars, girls, poker, instant messaging, and *Curb Your Enthusiasm*. Our house looked like a Louisville Slugger outlet, with bats of every size and color littering just about every room on the first and second floor. Intruders risked getting whacked by Sam's 33-inch, Manny Ramirez X-Bat.

We kept Sam in the dark while the issue was resolved. Like his dad, Sam lacks intellectual curiosity, hates sightseeing, and doesn't care much for travel in general. I feared that if we made the decision for him, and he later found out he'd missed the try-out, he might have wound up in a Sicilian jail for assaulting his parents.

I resisted the temptation to declare "Sam's going to North Carolina and that's that." Any veteran husband will tell you that this gets you nowhere. The trick was to make Marilou arrive at that inevitable conclusion on her own. So I started floating the question whenever we were around trusted friends and family members—people who knew Sam's passion for baseball. In the end, of course, even Sam's grandparents knew it was the right thing for him to do. Sicily, with all of its Greek ruins, has been there for centuries. Sicily would always be there.

So we went to Sicily and Sam went to Wilmington, North Carolina, and he did pretty well. He saw a high school kid who threw 98 miles per hour. He saw a lot of guys who'd be drafted in the spring of 2006. And he held his own. *Globe* baseball writer Gordon Edes left me a message saying that he'd spoken with a scout in Wilmington and the scout told him Sam was a Division I–caliber player. At the very least.

The night we returned from Sicily, we were preparing to go out for a family dinner when Sam got a call on his cell phone from a coach at Notre Dame. Boston College wanted to see him, also.

The tryout in Wilmington changed the course of Sam's life. He suddenly had chances to attend schools that would have had no interest in him if not for baseball. He had performed at his best against the best competition. And he had done it when Dad was on the other side of the Atlantic Ocean. Probably no coincidence.

September

SCHOOL STARTED ON THURSDAY, September 8, and Sam was out the door by 6:30 A.M. Marilou and I are blessed with kids who get up and go to school on their own. They learned this the hard way when they were young. I'd stand in Sam's doorway at dawn, toss a football into his bed, yell "Fummm-ble!!" in my best Keith Jackson voice, then dive on the mattress and scramble for the ball in a steroid-rage, playoffs-at-stake frenzy. Sam started getting up on his own after a few months of forced fumble treatments.

Sam's transcript and his (non)reading habits demonstrate that he is not the student his sisters were. Still, though he can often be lazy, he will never be late. I take some pride in this trait. Woody Allen noted that 90 percent of life is about showing up (and showing up on time), and I've worked in an on-time industry for more than three decades. Children pick up on that.

Sam had another incentive to get to school early, and it had nothing to do with girls, grades, or class registration. It's all about parking at Newton North. Space is limited and teachers and staff are guaranteed spots. Kids have to pay $180 per semester and enter a lottery in order to get a campus parking sticker. Early birds, however, can get coveted spots on Hull Street, and Sam knew that the $180 would be coming out of his pocket.

So most days he was out the door before either of his parents brushed their teeth.

Newton North, home to 2,200 students, is a monstrosity—a gigantic, confusing, worn, and almost windowless building. North has daunted many a freshman as he or she first tried to navigate its maze of corridors. Few parents spend enough time in the place to learn their way around, which is why student monitors serve as guides any time there's a back-to-school night for the folks. Built in 1973, urban legend holds that North was designed by someone who built prisons. The kids love that one.

The building was considered obsolete just a few years after it opened, and the class of '06 worked and played through three years of uncertainty while school and city officials debated the future of the structure. When Sam was a freshman, we were told that a scheduled renovation would force the school to transport underclassmen to other towns on buses. This caused a parental revolt only slightly less dramatic than the marches in Birmingham, Alabama, in the 1960s. After some lengthy and loud meetings, the relocation plan was scrapped. This led to a blue-ribbon, bipartisan, rainbow-coalition, ad hoc, multiflex-offense, fact-finding panel that debated the merits of building a new school versus renovating the existing building. State money was sought, architects were interviewed, and the process dragged through Sam's entire tenure at North. In January 2006, as projections for a new high school lurched toward $160 million, the principal, Jennifer Huntington, wrote, "Newton North is in terrible shape. The roof leaks; winter daily classroom temperatures range from 45 to 85 degrees, depending on classroom location; mold inhabits many parts of the school; the HVAC system has never worked properly. Students and faculty—and the city—need a new school."

In my narrow mind, I'd been embracing the costly procrastination so that the class of '06 would be allowed to get through four years without disruption or relocation. I knew that plans for the new building would obliterate Newton North's on-site, fenced-in baseball field and its cozy power alleys. Howard Ferguson Field and its fences had been good to Sam. And every high school athlete should enjoy the comfort of practicing and playing games on their own campus.

It was clear in the first couple of weeks of the 2005–2006 season that the North football team was going to be strong. The Tigers were loaded at the skill positions—all seniors who'd been part of Sam's world for twelve years. Sam had played as a freshman, and the team went 10-1 under the fine tutelage of one Tom Giusti, a gym teacher/football coach lifer who can work up a sweat just talking about football. Sam dropped out of football after the training camp of his sophomore year. He didn't like the game, even though he was built for it. His classmates went on to considerable success, and in the autumn of '05, North was ranked as one of the top ten teams in eastern Massachusetts.

While his classmates blocked and tackled, Sam was playing baseball. The college process was accelerating, but as his file of letters got thicker, his choices narrowed. By the middle of September, he'd trimmed his options to Boston College, Notre Dame, Holy Cross, and Connecticut.

His first official visit was to Boston College in mid-September. The campus is located less than three miles from our home, so BC didn't have to worry about any flight or hotel expenses. As we were leaving the house, I noticed Sam was wearing a T-shirt bearing some inane slogan across the back. Nice try. Go put on the polo. This turned out to be a good move. There were seven other recruits at the initial meeting and five of them wore polo-like shirts, most with the collars turned up.

I stuck around for the afternoon tour. The boys first listened to a strength and flexibility coach, who explained the rigors of training for Division I athletes. Clearly, the weight room was going to be homeroom for some of these guys. The strength coach was smart and energetic, and he really got my attention when he said, "If you get hurt, you're no good to us. You're here to play baseball."

This was different. Nobody had said that to Sam on visits to Williams, Tufts, Dartmouth, or Holy Cross.

I noticed another difference when listening to the young woman from the BC admissions office. She explained that BC gets 24,000 applicants for each freshman class of 2,250. In New England, this is known as the Flutie Factor. BC's been a hot school since Doug put it on the map with that Hail Mary pass in the Orange Bowl in 1984. It's not as selective as the Ivy League, but it's become increasingly difficult to gain admission. In my day, going to BC was like signing up for gym class. Certainly my 1971 BC application—routinely accepted by the board of admissions—would be quickly dismissed today.

I was taking notes while the admissions woman spoke, but the longer she talked the more I realized that gaining admission to Boston College was not going to be an issue for the young men on this official visit. Their transcripts had been run through the admissions department and all had been deemed admissible—or they would not have been invited for the visit. They were in. The admissions woman was not telling these guys what they had to do to qualify for Boston College, she was *selling* Boston College. Again, nothing like Sam's Williams College visit, when the admissions process dominated most of the interview. Hitting high school home runs is easy. Gaining admission to Williams is scaling Kilimanjaro.

It was time for me to leave after the admissions discussion. Sam was assigned a weekend roommate, a tall pitcher from central Massachusetts, and we agreed to meet the next afternoon when Sam had his exit interview with Coach Peter Hughes.

Coach Hughes is a no-nonsense guy. He and his wife have

five kids aged 1 to 8. He'd been adding on to his house, and I took this as an indication that he was staying at Boston College. He was investing in a plasma TV, always a sign that a guy is going to stick around. However, the BC baseball diamond doubles as a tailgating mecca on football weekends, and Boston College was set to play mighty Florida State on national television when Hughes was walking his recruits around campus. Acknowledging that there would be cars parked on the infield the next day, the embarrassed coach assured all the recruits that they'd be playing in a new, $15 million facility within a year or two of their arrival.

Marilou and I were still dubious about BC's interest in Sam, and more than once I said to the coach, "We just want to make sure that you are recruiting him and that he's not recruiting you."

"Absolutely," Hughes assured us while Sam was sitting right there. "We think he'll hit in the ACC."

Hughes kept talking about Sam's impatience. I could tell that Sam reminded him of himself a little. He said the only thing that worried him was Sam sitting and stewing on the bench for a year and a half. He was concerned that Sam couldn't handle waiting his turn to play. Mindful of other options, Hughes said, "Go to Holy Cross, Sam! Go ahead! You'll play right away! But if you come here you'll become a better player, and you'll play against the top competition in the country. You're just probably going to have to wait a little longer."

I remember something Sam had said to me earlier. He said he'd rather be the small fish in the big pond. He said he'd never had more fun than he did when he was 15 years old, batting in the number seven hole on a Legion team stacked with boys of 17, 18, and 19 years old. Bottom line: "Dad, I'd rather go to BC and suck than go to Holy Cross and suck."

Sam appeared to be in good shape when I picked him up Sunday morning. His roommate was still with him when I wheeled onto campus, and neither of them appeared to be hung over from the big Florida State game night. That said, any parents who think they know what their teenager is doing are delusional. We can't know everything, nor should we, yet I am amazed when I hear parents state, "I know my son and he would never do that. I know everything that he's up to."

No way. As a parent of a teen, your best bet is to set an example, show them the way, and then pray that nothing goes drastically wrong. Set up your household so that you are headquarters and all the kids want to hang out in your home. If this means a hot tub and Ping-Pong and plasma TV with high definition, go for it. Think of the expense as insurance against trouble. Keep the kids at home and out of cars as much as possible. But realize that when they are out of your sight, you have no idea what's going on. When he went off to college, my rules for Sam were the same as they were for the girls: don't get pregnant (or in Sam's case, don't get anybody pregnant), don't flunk out, and don't tell me what's really happening. I was there thirty years ago, and I know what this time of life is like; you're going to have to learn to get around the bumps and land mines by yourself.

The good news is that Sam is a man with a plan and he'd surrounded himself with kids who seem to be pretty levelheaded. Sometimes sports helps. At the 2006 Super Bowl in Detroit, the Seattle quarterback, Matt Hasselbeck, a product of Xaverian High School in Westwood (and later Boston College), told me, "I've said many times, had I not gone to Xaverian and been with the friends that I had there, I don't know that I ever would have earned a scholarship to college and I certainly wouldn't have been here. At a time when kids are getting into drinking and smoking and other stuff, my friends were into trying to earn a scholarship for sports. That's what Xaverian did for me. On Saturday night when some kids were going out to do who knows what, hang out at the movie parking lot, we were driving around looking for hoops to practice slam dunks on—nine-and-a-half-foot rims. That's what we did for fun. It was a great way to grow up and I feel very fortunate."

Of course, there's no such thing as an incident-free senior year, and I got one of those late-night phone calls on a warm Friday night just after high school classes started. Sam sounded alarmed. He said he'd been in a car accident and the police were there and could I come to the scene.

Your heart stops for a moment at times like this. Clearly, it was good that I was getting this call from my son and not from the authorities. Sam was able to tell me that no one was hurt. He was also upset with the people in the other vehicle involved in the crash, but I told him to just keep quiet and wait until I got there.

The incident took place at a notorious intersection about a half mile from our house. It's where the Massachusetts Turnpike meets Newton Corner, a confusing and circuitous web of roads that the locals have dubbed "the Circle of Death." There hasn't actually been a fatality there in many years, but it routinely ranks among the regional leaders in annual accident reports, and in our family we've always called it "the Rapids." If you can learn to navigate the Rapids, you'll be able to drive anywhere.

When I got to Newton Corner, Sam was sitting on a curb with one of his girlfriends. A fifty-something woman was standing over him, scolding him in Russian. She was with her husband and the police were on their way. I explained that I was Sam's dad. She said he had tried to "escape." That killed me. It turned out that the Russians had caused the minor crash because of their unfamiliarity with the unusual lane flow of the Rapids. I explained to her that Sam was not trying to escape when he continued through the intersection after the crash and pulled over at the next traffic light. She was having none of it. When the police arrived, I reminded Sam to be ever-polite with the men in blue. I also reminded him how much worse this would be if he'd had even one beer during the course of the evening. The police arrived, we exchanged papers, and Sam took his girlfriend home. Sam knew we wouldn't be paying for any body repairs on a 10-year-old Toyota Corolla, but he seemed relieved and comforted that I hadn't yelled at him.

I knew why. I was channeling a calm voice that I still had in my own head.

It didn't take long to find the entry in my high school diary. I knew it had happened on a weeknight during basketball season of my senior year. I'd been driving home from practice, a half mile from home—going the wrong way on a one-way street because it was a short cut and we did it every night—when I drove too fast across some black ice and sat powerless with my foot on the brake as our blue, four-door, Ford Custom 500 slowly skidded into a tree.

January 28. Thursday ... "I hit a tree coming home by the elementary school. Skidded. I was helpless and sat there and watched it happen. Told Dad. We looked at it. Told Ma. I'll remember how nice they were to me about this. Unreal. They both comforted me."

And so Sam Shaughnessy was spared the speech the night it happened to him. I hope he'll remember that when he gets the call late some night in 2041.

Sam the senior is nothing like his dad the senior in 1971. Sam doesn't read the newspaper. He hardly reads at all, except in front of the computer. He's a good athlete and has always had an easy time getting dates, or whatever they call it now. He hasn't had to work the way I worked, and as a result he has a totally unrealistic concept of money. He's seen us throw money at trouble to make it go away. He doesn't worry about ordering steak off the menu when we go out to eat, which is often. He's got a soft side (don't tell anyone, but he still sleeps with the stuffed Curious George he got when he was 4 years old). And he's also more generous and thoughtful than I was at the same age. In the spring of Sam's junior year, a few months after the epic Asian tsunami disaster, he walked into my office late one night and dropped $300 onto my keyboard as I was typing.

"Tsunami," he said. "You know what to do."

And then he was gone. Back to his computer in the hallway of our second floor. I sent the money to the Red Cross and we never talked about it again.

Newton North football played its annual "Friday Night Lights" game late in the month. The Tigers rolled over a surprisingly tough Norwood team while Marilou and I visited with assorted teachers, coaches, parents, and school administrators. Inadvertently, these are the nights when you find out about your kid. Under the rented lights, the athletic director, T. J. Williams, told me, "Sam came into my office with some last-minute paperwork today. I told him he's the highest-maintenance male in the high school. We've got a lot of girls like that, but he takes the cake for the boys."

Typical. There's never a semester without academic warnings, and everything from trash to homework gets done at the last minute.

My high school did not have a football team. Football was proposed at a town meeting early in the Kennedy administration, but the townsfolk voted against it and nobody ever missed it much. I remember occasionally going to watch football games at Groton School and Lawrence Academy, two prestigious prep schools in our town. One year, the Groton School boys somehow got to "borrow" our basketball cheerleaders during football season. I'm not quite sure how this happened, but they didn't have girls and we didn't have football and somebody decided it was a nifty idea. It gave us an incentive to go to some of the games.

In 1969, Senator Ted Kennedy came to visit his nephew, Joe Kennedy, who was a lineman for Milton Academy. This was just a few months after Chappaquiddick and Teddy had to have a driver. Nobody bothered him except me. I introduced myself as he stood on the sideline, and I'm pretty sure I offered him some of the Sugar Babies I'd bought at the concession stand. It was a moment.

The other thing I remember about those games was the spontaneous football played by little kids in the open spaces beyond the end zones: mini-footballs and mini-players with no pads, no rules, and nothing but joy in their shoes as they ran pass patterns and crashed into one another. Probably they don't do this in Odessa, Texas, or pockets of Ohio and West Virginia where high school football is more important than property taxes and school budgets. But in New England, you almost always see the little brothers of the ballplayers enjoying their own games and ignoring the heroics of the letter-sweater winners on the gridiron. At Newton North, the space behind the west end zone is most conducive to Nerf footballs. Like a lot of high schools, the football field is encircled by a quarter-mile track and the pole vault and long jump pits are carved inside the oval, beyond the west end zone. The pits double as sandboxes for tiny tots.

A few nights later, we were back at the high school for Senior Night—the annual evening in which parents of twelfth graders get the hell scared out of them by high school counselors. This is the night the counselors start talking about putting together a senior packet and making a game plan for the college application process. I have seen first-time attendees become physically ill during these sessions. The college application drill is made to sound only slightly less difficult than learning to play Rachmaninoff's Piano Concerto No. 2 without sheet music. Sam's counselor, Jim Burstein, did his best to calm the newcomers but made no attempt to downplay the stress of the next few months. He recommended that students apply to somewhere between eight and twelve colleges. He warned parents to make sure their kids applied to some "safety" schools and told them to prepare for the wounds of rejection letters. At one point, he mentioned that a Newton North student one year earlier had set what was believed to be the school record by applying to forty-seven colleges and universities. Naturally, the young man was accepted on early decision at his first choice.

We did not have personal collegiate counselors when I was a senior at Groton High School in 1970. There was a single guidance counselor and the objective clearly was "Aim low." I remember leaving the guidance counselor's office with applications to several nifty state colleges. I had Boston College on my list only because my dad had gone there and it was something of a lifelong plan. When my mom saw my pile of paperwork from Keene State, Framingham State, and Salem State, she said, "You'll apply to Holy Cross. That's where the LaVigne boys go and it's a good school like Boston College."

And that was that. I applied to Holy Cross and got accepted and one of those nice LaVigne boys walked me around the gated Worcester campus for an hour and I got a small scholarship and that was the end of the college search. It didn't require the time and preparation that went into the Marshall Plan. It was simple and relatively stress-free.

Eileen McNamara, a Pulitzer Prize–winning columnist for the *Globe,* has a story that speaks to the simplicity of those days. She was a bright student at North Cambridge Catholic High School in 1970 and planned to attend an Ivy League institution. When the guidance counselor/nun saw Columbia at the top of Eileen's college wish list, the kindly sister asked, "Dear, why would you want to go to school in South America?"

Aim low, remember?

Fast forward to Newton, Massachusetts, 2005, and you have

an alternate universe, one with parents prepping 6-year-old kids for their eventual ride to the Ivy League.

In the April 23, 2006, *New York Times,* Paula Marantz Cohen wrote, "Attending certain colleges these days is not just conspicuous consumption; it is also conspicuous achievement—accomplishments displayed as a sign of social status. And children are the favored vehicles... To fail at landing a seat in an elite college is to fall behind in the race that began with potty training ... The child-centered culture that has emerged the last several decades can be understood as an outgrowth of the creative self-expression of the 1960s. Parents came to see themselves as artists and their children as canvases or lumps of clay."

It's competitive, and it can be ugly and awful. It dominates too many conversations, and high school seniors around our town want to spit on the ground every time they are asked, "What are you going to do next year?"

Child-centered parent that I'd become, I initiated one call to a college for Sam. Harvard. Why not? I figured if Sam was good enough to play at Boston College or Notre Dame, he must be good enough to play at Harvard. Having navigated the Ivy minefield when Sarah was a senior, I knew the difficulty of any child being admitted to Harvard—never mind one with Sam's B-average transcript—but I wanted to make sure there was absolutely no chance before Sam committed anywhere else. My conversation with the Harvard coach was brief, blunt, and painful. We never even got to the issues of SATs and academic index. Sam had participated in several camps and tournaments at the Harvard baseball field and the coach was brutally honest with me.

"I didn't see anything special," he said.

Harsh and embarrassing for me. Necessary, too. Sam was almost 18. Time for Dad to step aside and let him do it on his own.

October

SAM TURNED 18 on the second day of October. I told him this meant he could enlist in the army. He told me he could now buy scratch tickets at 7-Eleven.

That weekend, the Red Sox and Yankees met at Fenway for the final games of the season, and I bought a pair of tickets for each game. Sam took the bus in from Newton for the Friday night series opener, and I was a little surprised when he showed up at the ballpark wearing his replica Red Sox jersey over a green hoodie. Replica jerseys are great for kids, but I've always held that there should be a cutoff for grownups. What's more pathetic than a 55-year-old man wearing his Curt Schilling jersey to the ballpark? Maybe you should stop when you are officially older than the youngest big league ballplayer. Whatever. Sam was still age-appropriate but not much longer, not in my book.

He looked big, especially when he followed me onto the field during batting practice and I introduced him to Reggie Jackson. Reggie hit 563 homers in the big leagues. He was the Bonds of his day. He was The Man when I started covering baseball in the mid-1970s and due to *ESPN Classic* and *Naked Gun* movies, Sam knew who he was. Sam also looked bigger than Reggie, which seemed hard to believe. Clearly, Reggie has gotten a little smaller since his playing days, but seeing Mr. October at the cage along-

side behemoths named Giambi, A-Rod, and Sheffield demonstrated how things have changed in major league baseball. The
summer of 2005 was the year of the big league steroid scandal
and nothing underscored the situation better than the scene at
the cage, as ballplayers—then and now—rubbed shoulders of a
decidedly different size.

For parents and coaches, steroids presented a new frontier.
Back in the day, our moms, dads, and coaches never wondered
about us abusing performance enhancers. When you really think
about it, what was available? Wonder Bread helped build strong
bodies twelve ways. Wheaties was the breakfast of champions.
Steak would make you big and strong. Orange juice gave you vi-
tamin C. Milk strengthened your bones. But there was no weight
training, no substance to swallow to make you big, strong,
and immortal. Instead, ads in the back pages of teen magazines
touted Charles Atlas and his program for building biceps to ward
off bullies who might kick sand in your face and make you look
bad at the beach. We worried about being 98-pound weaklings.
Sometimes, we even did pushups with television's inimitable
Jack La Lanne. But steroids? Never heard of 'em. Might as well
have been talking about ATMs, Gameboys, or the Internet.

In 2005, steroids were definitely something you discussed
with your teen athlete. I told Sam he didn't need any help with
muscle mass. He had plenty of natural strength. Getting bigger
would only make him more inflexible and less attractive to college baseball coaches. I knew he was going to get teased about
steroids because he hit the ball far and had a stocky physique.
But in the end, potential steroid use was just one more thing
that was out of my control—like teen drinking and drug abuse. I
could give all my speeches, but I was never going to really know
what Sam was doing. I hoped that meeting Reggie, a guy who hit
homers without chemical assistance, would help bring home the
message.

It was hard to get any words in once Reggie started talking to Sam. I tried whispering, "Sam, this guy hit three homers in a game once, too." Didn't matter. The old man had the young man's attention and, God bless him, Reggie talked to Sam about hitting. It's like a secret handshake: two guys comparing stances, demonstrating their trademark positioning of feet and arms. Reggie talked about weight shift and seeing the baseball. He told Sam he should try switch-hitting. He told Sam he was still a baby, not yet a man. He told him he'd still grow another two or three inches, and we both later laughed at that because it was looking like Sam was going to top out at five foot eleven, same as Reggie.

Sounding like Forrest Gump, Sam told me, "Reggie sure likes to use the F-word."

I laughed. When I saw Reggie the next day after the Yankees had clinched first place in the American League for the eighth straight season, I thanked him for making me look good in front of my son. It is one of the nicest things a man can do for another man.

On the night of Sam's eighteenth birthday, eight of us went to a restaurant called Fire + Ice in Cambridge. It's one of those trendy, teen-friendly places where you pick out raw meat and vegetables, buffet style, and give the bowl of uncooked food to a guy standing over a grill in the middle of the room, and later your food magically appears at your table. Sam inhaled a couple of plates of wings and steak tips, finished one of his sister's burgers, then gorged on chocolate cake. We all could do that when we were 18.

The best present he opened was from his oldest sister, Sarah —the Harvard girl. Typical of the oldest, Sarah is the prototype "good Do Bee," raise-your-hand-in-class, overachieving A student. In the classroom, she is ever prepared, thorough, and always engaged in the subject at hand. Teachers love Sarah. In the classroom, she is everything Sam is not, and we all know that it can be a nightmare to have an older sister setting high standards. She applied to six colleges when she was a senior at North and got into five. Her birthday gift to Sam was a framed copy of her rejection letter from Tufts. He loved that. It still has a special place of honor in his cluttered room.

A few days after the birthday bash, Marilou and I went to North for "Back to School Night," another event where pathetic parents navigate the impossible corridors of the characterless building. Sam predicted we'd like his calculus teacher and sure enough, the guy was young and loved sports and told riddles. He had even run track at Boston College. Sam predicted that Mr. Wallace would be wearing a tie, but it was a ruse. The math man apparently liked to dress down. He'd written a slogan on his blackboard and I could hardly take my eyes off it the whole time he was talking. It read, "Somewhere in the world someone is training when you are not. When you face them, they will win."

It reminded me of Larry Bird and his high school friend Beezer Carnes. Larry always talked about how he and his friends would go to the gym early, before school, and shoot free throws on their own. Beezer was too lazy and routinely skipped the sessions. Then one night, at the end of a game, Beezer missed a couple of free throws and lost an important game. Larry never said anything to Beezer. He just looked at him and they both knew. Anyway, I liked the math teacher.

The physics teacher also seemed cool. He said one of Sam's home runs hit his car in third lot in the previous spring. He also said Sam showed interest in physics. It figured. There's lots of physics in baseball—the rotation of a curveball, the force of a wood bat going through the strike zone and connecting with a hard object traveling eighty-five miles an hour. Math and physics are interesting topics if you like to hit. Ted Williams could have told you that.

Sam's business teacher seemed pleased to hear that Sam had poured his life's savings ($3,200) into 180 shares of JetBlue. This was not Sam's first foray into the market, nor was it his first time buying airline stock. The day after 9/11, when he was only 13 years old, Sam—with help from his stockbroker uncle Bill—put a couple of hundred bucks into American and United Airlines. Sam thought the stock most definitely would go up. Unfortunately, the stock tanked. He's pretty sure JetBlue will make things right and he's got a plan to dump if his initial losses reach $200. All this makes the Carroll School of Management at Boston College seem like a good idea.

In mid-month we got the hot tub running, an annual autumn ritual. An expensive toy, the tub was purchased when the girls started high school and has been handy for kids in need of relaxation after preseason practices. Of course, there've been times when we wondered, "What were we thinking?" as teen girls in skimpy swimsuits came to visit Sam. When Sam was about 14, his sisters would tease him, saying, "Sam, those girls don't even like you. They're just coming over to use the hot tub!" His response went something like "What's your point?" I thought about getting him one of those Hugh Hefner smoking jackets, but everyone thought it was a dumb idea.

I got a form letter from my cousin Mickey and his wife. They'd started a scholarship fund in the memory of Michael. It read, in part, "How wonderful it was to watch Michael as he grew on the fields and playgrounds of Westford. It is easy to remember Michael's enthusiasm for sports and friends; to see his pride as he competed for Westford Academy and earned a scholarship to play college football. We have received many caring and supportive notes, including those from other school teams, athletes, and coaches. They serve to remind us that while our children compete on the field, they (and we) are part of a larger community that can pull together during difficult times . . . As we drive through town and see children playing on the fields, it is easy to remember how Michael enjoyed his times playing sports. We should all cherish and nurture the enthusiasm that is childhood, and hug our kids just a bit more often."

I sent a check the next day and made a note to myself to call Mickey. And to give Sam a big hug.

Then came the official visit to Notre Dame.

Sam had been reluctant about the whole thing. We all knew he liked Boston College, and it was almost as if he was afraid to go to South Bend because he might like it too much and that would make his decision more difficult. Just about every other school was off the table by this time. None of us knew the process would move this swiftly, but because Sam was a spring sport athlete, there was no more chance for college scouting. Like all the other baseball players, Sam's resumé was complete. Good thing he had had a strong junior year.

Which brings us to the topic of showcases—moneymaking meat markets of high school players, where coaches allegedly show up and identify players they'll consider offering scholarships to. In this century, when you are a parent of a talented high school athlete, you write out a check for several hundred bucks and send your child to a showcase, hopefully somewhere near home. These things certainly didn't exist when Bill Shaughnessy was a high school baseball stud in Groton, Massachusetts. There was a guy in Groton who was supposed to be a baseball scout. He had white hair and seemed to be a million years old. I never saw him at one of Bill's games, and there was no professional contract waiting when Bill finished high school. It seemed to me that no one ever really scouted my big brother.

Bill went away to tiny Nichols College in southeastern Massachusetts and played four strong seasons as a power-hitting corner-outfielder for the Bisons. When his college career was over, he got drafted . . . by Uncle Sam. This was not exactly what he had in mind, but it was 1969 and the mandatory draft was in full bloom. Baseball bailed him out, however, and quite possibly saved his life. There were teams on the U.S. military bases and some general decided that he wanted Bill to play for his team in Germany, so William J. Shaughnessy Jr. rode out the Vietnam War playing outfield in Heidelberg. When his service was up, he went to spring training and tried out for the Phillies, but they knew he was already in his mid-twenties and wasn't worth signing.

Was my brother good enough to play big league ball, or even minor league baseball? We'll never know. He'll never know. He's one of the hundreds of thousands of guys on couches and barstools who all believe they could have been contenders if only they'd gotten a fair shot. America is populated and sometimes plagued by these men. They are often the ones you hear screaming loudest from the bleachers at Little League or high school games. There are surveys to prove this. Posed with the question "If not for an injury or bad coaching or getting overlooked, could you have played professionally in the sport of your choice?" three-quarters of men will answer in the affirmative. And a lot of these men are the ones coaching your kids.

In 2006, being "overlooked" can no longer be an excuse. Professional scouting is far more extensive and sophisticated than it was forty years ago. There is video and Internet and news coverage that did not exist in my youth. And there are the showcases, where all the talented young players get to show their wares.

Sam went to his first showcase when he was 15, and attended about a dozen of them before he was a senior in high school. The drill was fairly standard. Players were timed in the 60-yard dash then sent to defensive stations where they fielded and made throws. Hitters were given six to ten batting practice swings. Then they played games, sometimes with simulated rules — always stacked to illuminate the strengths and weaknesses of the pitcher. Every hitter starts with a 1-1 count.

Parents could often be seen filming these tryouts, or charting pitches from the stands, but the only people who mattered really were the college and pro scouts—carrying stopwatches, wearing sunglasses and ball caps pulled down over their eyes, quietly taking notes. Sam was not a showcase animal. He was faster than most players, running a 6.9 as his best time, but there were plenty of kids considerably faster. Sam's arm was below average, and many of the scouts would take him off their lists when they saw his lame throws from the outfield. He was saved by his bat speed, which appeared to make him a potential Division I prospect. Scouts did not consider performance at the showcases, only tools. You could strike out, as long as you looked good striking out.

After writing yet another multi-hundred-dollar check to enroll Sam in another one of these events, I told him, "Sam, if none of the schools want you after all this, it'll mean you truly suck. You're certainly never going to be able to say, 'I could have been great, but nobody ever saw me.'"

"Thanks, Dad," Sam mumbled, smiling.

I could tease him about it because we both knew there were schools already interested.

Notre Dame assistant coach Terry Rooney called almost every week until the visit. Only 31 years old, Rooney seemed to love Notre Dame more than any man alive. He used a lot of exclamation points in his e-mails. He and the rest of the ND staff were fastidious about NCAA regulations and potential violations. The rules state that coaches can make only one phone contact per week (yet they can text message anytime they want). In one instance, I called Rooney, left a number, and got no return call. When I reached him later in the day, he explained that he had been unable to call me back even though he knew I was home waiting, because he had talked to Sam the night before. Another ND assistant told me that they faced a $25,000 fine if they were caught breaking any NCAA rules. "That's almost as much as we make," he added.

We went to Notre Dame ("Don't bump into any cows," BC's Hughes advised Sam on the eve of the visit) on the weekend of October 14, which happened to be the weekend that the Irish were playing USC. It's a rivalry on a par with Army-Navy, Texas-Oklahoma, or Michigan–Ohio State, but in 2005 it was bigger than usual because the Irish were in the early days of an exciting new era under head coach Charlie Weis, while the Trojans were two-time defending national champs, boasting two Heisman trophy winners, and working on a twenty-seven-game winning streak.

In other words, not a bad weekend to bring recruits to campus.

I was already in Chicago, working the American League Championship Series between the White Sox and Angels, so I rented a car and picked up Sam and Marilou at O'Hare just before noon on Friday. The tollway road toward Indiana was clogged with construction and trucks, and it took us three hours to make the 120-mile trip. Looking at Sam in the rearview mirror of the Avis Buick ("Sweet ride, Dad," was his opening salute at O'Hare), I envisioned a cartoon bubble over his head with the words, "I can walk to BC from home in twenty minutes. Why would I want to go through all of this just to go play baseball in college?"

After we paid our final toll, Sam called the coach and said we would meet them at the field in about ten minutes. Then I pulled over so he could change into his official recruiting outfit: black polo shirt and khakis.

We pulled into beautiful Frank Eck Stadium, not far from the 80,000-seat bowl where the Irish would play Southern Cal the next day. Head coach Paul Mainieri was there to shake hands, and two of his assistants handed us papers we would need for the weekend. Then they walked us into an indoor batting cage adjacent to the stadium. Sam was told that he could hit here anytime he wanted. He'd have a pass code to open the door, and the building was always open to the baseball players only. I pictured Sam walking through the darkness to the facility at 3 A.M. after striking out a couple of times earlier in the day.

The clubhouse was better equipped than most minor league clubhouses. There was a big-screen television, and all the players had their own stalls. In Mainieri's office, somebody had made a great effort to show off Notre Dame's baseball uniforms and equipment. It looked like something you'd see in the window of a sporting goods store. Adidas is the official supplier of all Notre Dame teams, and one can see that the enormous popularity of the football program has been very good for all other sports. The vast spread of sporting goods was ridiculous: seven varieties of hats, a series of different-colored uniform tops and warm-up jackets. Gloves by Rawlings—with players' names sewn into the leather. Bats by Louisville Slugger. Letter jackets. Rings.

"You'll get all of this," said the coach.

These guys had it down. Perfect weather. The biggest college football game of the year. Incredible facilities and school garb. They'd even arranged to have the wind blowing out to right field. At 330 feet down the line, it didn't look like too much of a poke.

On our tour, we were accompanied by four other recruits and their parents. After eating sandwiches and conversing a bit with the coaches, we went into the football stadium where 42,000 were gathering for perhaps the largest collegiate pep rally in American history. The master of ceremonies was Dan Ruettiger, AKA "Rudy" of motion picture fame. Joe Montana, Tim Brown, and Chris Zorich spoke. Rudy was pretty animated. The ND baseball players thought he might have been tailgating a day early. I wondered what he does for a living now. When he fills out his tax forms and gets to the box labeled "occupation," does he write "Rudy"?

They took us to dinner at a place called Parisi's. Watching the coach and his wife make their way through the restaurant reminded me of Ray Liotta entering the nightclub through the kitchen in *Goodfellas*. These people knew everybody. This was a coach who was never leaving Notre Dame. That was for sure.

We ate family style, which was appropriate since the coach's dad, Doc Mainieri, another coach-lifer, entertained us with stories of coaching Red Sox manager Terry Francona in the Cape League and of taking his family to Italy, where he also coached baseball. Assistant Coach Rooney's parents were also at the table: his dad went to Holy Cross, his mom to Boston College. Mainieri's good friend Jim Hendry, General Manager of the Chicago Cubs, dined with us and talked to the recruits. I reminded Sam that Hendry was the guy who traded for Nomar Garciaparra in Boston's magical summer of 2004. Digger Phelps and Seattle lefty Jamie Moyer stopped by to talk with the boys. Sam later said he wanted to ask Moyer about pitching to Manny Ramirez because Manny had hit nine or ten homers off him. Regrettably, Sam eschewed the opportunity.

After dinner, Sam went to the dorms with the ballplayers, and we retired to the Hampton Inn, guests of Notre Dame baseball. When my head hit the pillow, the Notre Dame fight song (who ever knew it had actual words?) was still pounding between my ears.

This was different. New territory all around for the Shaughnessy family. As a kid, I'd watched Ronald Reagan as the Gipper on black-and-white TV and learned to play the Notre Dame fight song on our upright piano. I'd read old Grantland Rice stories. But nothing like this ever happened to anybody who played high school sports in Groton in the 1960s.

The next morning, we were back on campus, meeting Sam

and his host player at 8:15 A.M. Sam's roommate was a junior catcher from Indiana. He'd been drafted by the White Sox out of high school and told Sam he hoped to get drafted again and go to the minors after the upcoming season.

They took us into the bubble, where they practice during the winter, then we saw the weight room that had been dedicated a day earlier and was, according to everyone who spoke, the best college weight room in the country. After listening to the strength coach, we absorbed a one-hour lecture from a campus professor/local judge who had put all six of his children through Notre Dame. This stately man said Notre Dame would make each of them the "best student, best baseball player, and best person they can be." Then the head of alumni clubs told us that there are 216 Notre Dame clubs around the world. With each person, the message was pretty much the same: "If you want to be good, go someplace else. If you want to be great, come to Notre Dame."

Recruiter/coach Rooney especially liked this theme. His other favorites were "The easy decision isn't always the best decision" and "This is what Notre Dame is all about."

Marilou, a native of Michigan and a Michigan State grad, was buying the whole package, talking up "the great Midwest," when a coach said something that stopped her in mid-praise. We were walking around campus, near the golden dome, and we'd just taken a photo of Sam—arms raised—standing in front of Touchdown Jesus on the library building, when she first heard the word *parietals*. I knew exactly what the coach was talking about, but my wife and some of the other parents didn't recognize the term. It means no overnight visits by members of the opposite sex. Girls would have to be out of the rooms by a specified hour. This rule was taken very seriously at Notre Dame. Ballplayers told Sam that a parietals violation was worse than getting caught drinking. Ouch.

My wife was appalled. "Sleeping over? That's what college is for," she mumbled as we passed Joe Montana strolling through the perfect grounds.

"What are you, some state school slut?" I asked, feigning surprise. "This isn't the northeast. Why do you think the Democrats keep losing elections?"

There were several other indications that we were no longer in John Kerry Country. Graphic anti-abortion displays (a sign featuring several mini-school buses dedicated to all the murdered children) lined the streets en route to the school, and there was an abundance of anti-abortion literature on campus. Sam's mom was amazed. Sam noticed none of it. He couldn't stop thinking about the opportunity to hit at three in the morning.

Next on tap was the Game of the Century. It had to be impressive for Sam and the other recruits to be standing on the field as the Irish, wearing their green jerseys, came out of the tunnel in front of 80,000 fans. A truly spectacular football game unfolded over the next four hours, and for a couple of seconds it appeared Notre Dame had upset the national champs. A few thousand students hurdled the clay-brick walls and stormed the gridiron prematurely, but they were herded back to their seats and USC won on a one-yard keeper by Heisman Trophy winner Matt Leinart, with three seconds left on the clock.

We didn't see Sam again until the next morning when we had our exit interview/breakfast with the coaching staff. It lasted one hour. We were assured that Sam would be admitted if he signed a letter of intent in November. Mainieri said he could not promise playing time but told Sam he thought they could use him right away if he played well in the fall and spring scrimmages. He told Sam he knew Coach Hughes at Boston College and that either school was a good choice. They offered Sam a small scholarship, apologized for not having more, but noted that college baseball gets only 11.7 total scholarships, and most of it goes to pitchers and skill position players. Finally, Mainieri gently reminded

Sam that if he declined their offer, Notre Dame needed to skip down its list and go after another hitter. They had a boy scheduled to visit in two weeks when the Irish played Tennessee. No pressure, but they needed to know sometime during the upcoming week. Again, Sam was told that if he wanted to be great, he'd go to Notre Dame. If he wanted to settle for good, he'd go someplace else.

We said goodbye to the coaches and went to the bookstore before driving to Chicago. Sam tried on a couple of ND hats but did not buy. Too much commitment.

Back in the car, mercifully back in jeans instead of khakis, Sam said, "Dad, I feel like you're going to be disappointed if I don't go to Notre Dame."

Not what I wanted to hear. This decision couldn't be based on how his parents might react.

"Sam, I'm sorry if I gave you that impression. You've got two great choices here. There is no wrong decision and we are happy no matter what. Your call."

He put the headphones on while we drove to O'Hare. I dropped them off, went back to my Chicago hotel, and later called Marilou to see how they were doing at the airport.

"There was a long line at security," she started. "Sam said, 'I could have walked to BC while I waited to get on the plane.'"

I returned to Boston on Monday, waiting to find out who the White Sox were going to play in the World Series. Sam came home from school and said he'd talked to one teacher and a lot of his friends about the decision. Many of them were telling him he should definitely leave home and go to Notre Dame. He'd also made a call to Coach Hughes at Boston College and came away thinking he might not have to wait a year and a half before getting to bat for the Eagles. Hughes told him they hadn't yet signed any position players. Sam asked about the new facilities. Hughes said they'd eventually have a twenty-four-hour hitting building, just like Notre Dame.

Not much happened for a couple of days. Sam went to hit at the cages every day, but he wasn't saying much about it or asking any more questions. He did not seem burdened.

I was surprised. I'd expected him to come home Sunday night and announce he was going to Boston College. I kept thinking about what a lucky boy he was. He'd worked at this, sure, but baseball was giving him a choice of two great academic institutions.

Michael LaVigne, one of the famed LaVigne boys of Groton and Holy Cross, stopped by the house Tuesday night. The La-Vignes' house was in the middle of downtown Groton, and there always seemed to be a football game being played on the enormous front lawn. There were five LaVigne kids, four boys and one girl. They could field an entire infield for a Little League game. Their dad was a radiologist who had gone to Holy Cross, and they went to Mass every Sunday and attended private schools during the week. When Michael was a senior, he broke ranks with family tradition and applied to Harvard, and he remembered hearing his dad on the phone telling a friend, "Michael is applying to Harvard. I don't know how he's planning on paying for it, but he's applying there." Alas, Michael went to Holy Cross with his three brothers and sister.

Michael is an assistant soccer coach at Boston College and a full-time housepainter by trade. He was Sam's boss the summer before senior year, and no high school kid ever had a better deal than Sam Shaughnessy under Mike LaVigne. Mike was okay whenever Sam had to skip work because of a baseball showcase or leave early on a game night. Plus, Mike hired an all-girl crew of soccer players, which certainly made Sam happy. The crew enjoyed Aloha Fridays (off at noon), and everybody got the day off the day after the Rolling Stones played Fenway Park because Michael had partied too hard the night before. October 20 is forever a paid holiday for the LaVigne crew because that's the day the Red Sox beat the Yankees in game seven to close out the greatest comeback in baseball history. Mike had to get permission from BC before hiring Sam because it could have been an NCAA violation. Turned out it was okay—Mike was a family friend who had known the recruit since birth.

Michael stood around our kitchen for a couple of hours on that weeknight after the BC visit. Sam and Marilou made plans to watch Mike at work when the BC women played Virginia on Thursday afternoon.

Wednesday, Sam came home from hitting and asked if I wanted to go eat at the Golden Star. I took this as a sign he was ready to tell us which school he wanted. The Star is a dark, cheap, quiet Chinese restaurant about two miles from our house. I've been going there for thirty years, and Marilou remembers drinking cheap wine there the night we bought our first house. It's been the site of many family discussions—the staff at the Star always gave us the round table in a corner by the door. Dozens of times we've eaten there while one or more of the kids was still dirty and sweating, wearing the uniform from a game just played. The Star is run by a group of Chinese men with American names: Vinny, Chuck, Jack, Billy, Paul, George, and Huey. Huey worked behind bar for several decades and I loved to stop by for a Mai Tai and some General Gau's chicken on the way to Sam's summer night games (I once asked one of the waiters for some history on General Gau and was told, "He was one of our generals"). A Cliff-and-Norm-esque gang of regular patrons sits at the bar nightly, watching *Jeopardy,* then switching to whatever game is on the TV. There's a rickety phone booth under the television and whenever it rings at night, one of the regulars will hop off his stool, turn, and shout, "Is everybody here?" The owners at the Star prefer cash over credit cards and have been known to ring up $0.00 when taking cash for a dinner tab. Sam thinks they're running a cockfight operation downstairs.

As Sam and I were heading out the door for the Star, the

phone rang. It was Coach Rooney, calling from Notre Dame. When I gave the phone to Sam, I scribbled a message on a kitchen pad—"Don't commit." After they spoke, Sam and I were off to the Star and Marilou met us . . .

Nothing.

"I haven't really thought much about it today," said Sam.

That night, Marilou and I both scratched our heads. We were feeling a little edgy. We had both wanted him to see Notre Dame, and there were moments when it seemed like the best idea, but the longer this went on the more it seemed he might actually go there and we were the ones getting homesick. I'd wanted Sam to see everything there was to offer and I'd wanted him to think long and hard about it. He was doing that, and now I was getting selfish. If he went to Notre Dame, I'd hardly ever get to see him play. Gulp.

It was the same obtuse routine when he came home from school on Thursday.

"What's up," I asked, fetching.

"Not much," he said, sitting down at the computer in the hall-way. "We still going to watch Mike's game?"

"I guess."

The three of us got in the car and made the short drive to the Boston College campus. I drove. Sam rode shotgun with Marilou in the back. We were heading up Beacon Street bound for Centre Street, which would take us to the field, when Sam made a small motion with his hand, softly urging me to turn right into the Conte Forum sports complex.

Infinitely understated.

Typical Sam. He's never been one for loud noise or theatrics.

But this was it. I knew. The small wave of his hand was the signal that he had made his decision. He wanted to go see Coach Hughes in the BC offices.

I drove to the front of Conte Forum, beached the car in a fifteen-minute parking spot, turned to Sam, and said, "You want to go up?"

He nodded.

The three of us went into the building, rode the elevator to the fourth floor, and made the long walk to the baseball offices. Without speaking.

When we got to Hughes's office, I could see the coach behind the glass, typing at his computer. Sam went in alone while we stayed by the reception desk. I could see them smiling and shaking hands. Hughes put his arm on Sam's shoulder and called us into the office. When we walked in, Hughes told us Sam made a good decision.

"What is it?" we asked.

Hughes laughed at us.

"Boston College."

We sat down and I asked Sam to tell Coach what made him decide. What was the deal breaker?

"Two signs," he told Hughes. "I noticed you switched to De-Marini bats, which I love. I could be a spokesman for DeMarini bats. And the second sign was your car. When I was on my visit to BC, my host player pointed out your car. Cadillac DeVille. I love the Cadillac DeVille."

Coach walked us to our car. He said they'd be FedExing the letter of intent on November 9. Sam was an Eagle.

We went to the BC women's soccer game, where Sam's sister Kate joined us ("Way to go, Big Cat," she told him). She took him to the Boston College bookstore. A ceremonial pilgrimage. They got the BC hat, the BC sweatshirt, and the BC keychain/bottle opener. They even picked up the cornball "Boston College Mom" coffee mug.

Kate and Sarah had plans to meet that night to drive to Worcester to see Bruce Springsteen. Marilou picked Sarah up at school and would not tell her what Sam had decided. When they pulled up out front, Sarah ran into the house, saw Sam in his BC garb, and jumped into his arms. He caught the catcher.

There it was. On the first anniversary of the Red Sox win over the Yankees—an official holiday for the LaVigne painting crew and for much of New England—Sam made the biggest decision of his first eighteen years. And all because of DeMarini bats and a Cadillac DeVille.

November

MAILINGS FROM THE HIGH SCHOOL arrived with some regularity. For the past eight years, we've had dozens of missives addressed "To the parents of Sam [or Sarah or Kate] Shaughnessy." The benign ones promote upcoming events and dates to remember. Ever vigilant and sensitive to the student body's needs, sometimes the memos addressed a recent local or national tragedy. We got a note after 9/11, and there's always a mailing if there's been any kind of hate graffiti scrawled on campus. Parking regulations have required a torrent of mailings.

And then there are the academic warnings . . .

Sam does not have a C on his transcript, but he's yet to get through a semester without at least one warning. The usual problems cited: "fails to participate in class," "needs to improve on quizzes," and the ever appropriate "can do better." Marilou thought about offering Sam a hundred bucks if he could somehow go just one term without a warning, but we agreed that would be a tad indulgent.

In the autumn of '05, Sam got his warning in English.

"That's just the way Sam has to do it," said his mom. "Just like when he's hitting. He's a 3-2 kid. He's always 3-2."

From trash to trigonometry, the truth of the remark was undeniable, but what was most stunning was Marilou's sudden ability to use baseball language to explain a fundamental aspect of our son's personality. This is the woman who knows almost nothing about sports. This is the woman who attended Michigan State when Magic Johnson was there and never saw him play a minute of college basketball (my colleague Bob Ryan has never gotten over that one). When I got her a coveted ticket to watch the Lakers at the old Forum in Inglewood, California, she brought *The Rise and Fall of the Third Reich* to her front row seat—a little light reading in between skyhooks by Kareem Abdul-Jabbar. She usually brings knitting to Sam's games. A couple of summers ago, after Sam won a Legion game with a walkoff homer, she called me and said, "Sam hit a home run and everybody said it was a 'walker' or something like that." That was a year before she accompanied me to a party at the Kenmore Square Commonwealth Hotel, hosted by new Dodger owner Frank McCourt, a native of South Boston, when the Dodgers played their first series at Fenway Park in the summer of 2004. McCourt brought Vin Scully, Tom Lasorda, and all the Dodger tradition with him. In this context, it was slightly unsettling to look across the gathering and see my wife talking to Sandy Koufax. What a waste. Hundreds of partygoers would have traded their firstborns for a chance to speak with mound royalty, and there was Marilou chatting up Koufax, oblivious to the fact that she was speaking with a legitimate baseball god.

"What a handsome older man," she noted.

Sigh.

Sam *is* always 3-2 in life. His teachers, coaches, friends, and parents are all used to it by now.

In the middle of football season, I was disappointed to open a mailing from the high school principal that indicated that the annual "Powder Puff" football game was being canceled.

Rats. I love the Powder Puff football game. It was part of

Shaughnessy family folklore. We first became aware of the ritual when Sarah was a junior at North. Through the years, the Powder Puff game featured junior class girls versus senior class girls in a not-so-friendly game of touch football. Class pride was at stake—bragging rights that carried through graduation and beyond. The girls held informal practices and varsity football boys served as coaches. Fueled by alcohol, the games started to grow out of control after the turn of the century, which is when school authorities first hired professional referees to keep the games under control.

In 2001, when Sarah was a senior and Kate a junior, the competition peaked. On the morning of the game, the well-trained football girls convened at a practice site, decorated their cars with boasts of class supremacy, smeared war paint on their faces, cranked car stereos to 11, and drove to the field in a proud procession. The seniors played "Eye of the Tiger" when they poured out of their cars and marched toward the sideline.

Sam was an eighth grader that year, and he and I went to watch our girls go eyeblack to eyeblack. I felt like the president of the United States at the Army-Navy game, required to switch sides at halftime. It was impressive to see real MIAA officials with their zebra shirts and whistles. None of the players appeared to be inebriated. Not so impressive was the conduct of my daughters. Sports competition has always brought out the innate baggage of sisterhood. It was unfortunate that my daughters had been assigned to play in the trenches. This meant they could line up against one another on every play. Trouble—remember Dottie and Kit in *A League of Their Own*?

You could see it escalate. Sarah would be in charge of blocking Kate when the seniors were on offense, and Kate was trying to contain Sarah when the juniors had the ball. On each series of downs, there was more agitation, more grabbing and pulling. Before you could say "WWF," my daughters were rolling around on the ground, kicking, gouging, and cursing at one another. The referee, who did not know they were related, ejected both. A couple of Carla Everetts. Like I said, instant family folklore.

It was the drinking and these kinds of episodes that brought that flyer to our home in the fall of 2005. Under the hideous headline SAYING NO TO THE "POWDER PUFF" GAME, Principal Huntington wrote, "In years past the game got out of hand and even resulted in some injuries. In an effort to have more control, we tried monitoring the game and the crowds and even got professional referees. Despite our best efforts last year, emotions ran high and got out of hand. Cars were damaged and students were hurt, which caused us to cancel the pep rally. After much thought, we have decided to cancel the game altogether as a school sponsored activity."

No more Powder Puff . . . the end of an era . . . another high school tradition banished in the name of safety and progress.

What made the Powder Puff missive particularly disturbing was the fact that it came on the heels of the cancellation of Halloween at our local elementary school. The squashing of Halloween by our well-intentioned school principal made national news. *Good Morning America*, Fox News, NPR, and the *Christian Science Monitor* were just a few of the national outlets that reported the sad story.

Underwood principal David Castelline, who forever will be a hero in the Shaughnessy household after the delicate manner in which he handled Kate's bout with leukemia, stepped into a minefield when he ceded to the wishes of a few parents and teachers who complained about elementary school teachers dressing up in costumes on Halloween. Teachers told Castelline that at least three students said they were not coming to school on Halloween because celebration of the day offended their religious beliefs. The principal's letter read, "The traditional practices we have engaged in regarding Halloween are offensive to the religious beliefs of some members of our community. In our continuous attempts to make our school a place where all members feel welcome, we will not be celebrating Halloween in school this year."

Yikes. Another tradition bites the dust in the interest of political correctness. I wondered what would happen if children who live in vegetarian households complained about Thanksgiving? And what about the school-sanctioned Gay/Straight Alliance at North? One day a year is designed as ToBGLADay (Transgender, Bisexual, Gay, Lesbian Alliance), a presentation of programs by the Gay/Straight Alliance. In 2005, Newton North's ToBGLADay program included a discussion with transgender people and a documentary film exploring the way gay issues are taught in elementary schools. Some might find this offensive or against their religion, but those voices will not be heard. Marilou says I should shut up about this and probably she is right.

November's mail also brought Sam's registration letter from the Selective Service System. The letter explained that he must register for military service and failure to do so might result in imprisonment for up to five years and/or a fine of not more than $250,000. He could register online, over the phone, or by mailing the form back to Palatine, Illinois. Marilou handled just about all of Sam's paperwork, but she refused to be involved in this process.

"I'm not doing it," she said, dumping the letter on my belly as I lay reading in bed. "You do it. Mothers can't be part of that."

That took me back to 1969, when my brother graduated from college and instantly became eligible for the draft. My dad was a World War II veteran, winner of a Purple Heart after getting wounded by shrapnel in Germany. Bill Shaughnessy Sr. didn't want to see his son go off to war, but he wasn't having any part of the conversation when my mother started talking about Bill Jr. going to Canada. Being Irish, we didn't hear a lot of raised voices in our home through the years—it was always easier to pretend nothing was wrong—but I remember Mom and Dad getting into it over this one. I was a sophomore in high school, and my mom was already keeping copious records of my asthma treatments to make sure I'd get a medical deferment. Brother Bill had no outs. Vietnam was in full fury, and he was off to basic training a few months after getting his college diploma. Fortunately, his time overseas was spent in Germany, throwing baseballs instead of grenades.

The antiwar movement was in full bloom during my high school days. We watched Uncle Walter Cronkite on the nightly news and noted his disapproval. We let our hair grow, played "Ohio" on our turntables, and pasted war protest photos on the school bulletin board. But ours was a symbolic dissent. Nobody was burning American flags in Groton, not with Fort Devens next door to our little town.

Folks from the Fort drifted into our lives with some regularity. I still remember the southern drawl and high energy of a U.S. Army general's wife who served as a student teacher when I was a senior. She was at once inspirational and kooky. Eager to assimilate into our world, she accepted an invitation to bring the general to the school prom, and our dates got to dance with the general when the orchestra instructed us to change partners during one of the slow numbers. When my date returned from her twirl with the general, she breathlessly remarked, "The general was great. A regular guy. We just talked about regular stuff."

Hearing this, my friend Doug Richardson sighed and said, "What did you think he was going to talk about—napalm?"

Inspired by the general's wife, Doug went to the Citadel, and today he is a one-star general living in Tacoma.

There weren't a lot of young people with an eye on military service in those days. My name went into the draft lottery in 1972 and my birthday put me at dangerously low number 33.

Fortunately, Richard Nixon stopped the draft before our time came and my mom never needed to unleash my asthma files on the Selective Service Board. But I still carry my draft card. It was issued August 6, 1971; they told us to keep it on our person at all times and no one ever rescinded the order. It says I'm six foot one and 155 pounds (ah, the golden days), classified as 1-A.

Sam made his military registration phone call on a Sunday while our nation was knee deep in another war that was wildly unpopular at home. I knew he was hoping to get drafted . . . by the Orioles or Brewers or Pirates. Kids today don't worry about getting a call from Uncle Sam.

At this same time, his English class was reading *The Things They Carried*, the popular book written by Vietnam War veteran Tim O'Brien. For an assignment inspired by the book, students were required to write a story using personal backpack contents to describe themselves in the third person.

An excerpt from Sam's essay:

Newton North student Sam Shaughnessy carries an assortment of items he sees as necessary for his very existence. The items he carries do not weigh a great deal in the metric system. What he carries cannot truly be weighed in units. Because to Sam, his baseball bat weighs more than his car, and he drives a pretty big sedan . . . Sam carries his sense of humor everywhere he goes. Humor represents negative weight; it lightens the load of all the heavy things a person humps . . . Sam carries a baseball bat. A bat made from rock maple wood. Unfinished, yet more polished than anything he owns. The lower half of the bat is filthy, sticky and stinky with pine tar. But it smells good to Sam. In fact, he loves the smell of pine tar, especially in the morning. It smells like victory. The bat is 33 inches long and weighs 30 and a half ounces. Sam carries this bat around everywhere, both literally and metaphorically. The bat he carries is the most important tangible and intangible item he carries. His bat is his respect. It is what brings out his greatest talent, because when Sam is standing in the batter's box, holding that bat, everyone on the field and watching the game looks at him with respect, even though he is wearing suggestively tight bright white pants. The bat he carries enabled him to be accepted into a college that would not accept him for the grades and SAT scores that he carries. It is ironic that his bat was more important for getting into college than his SAT tutoring, than his sleepless month slaving away at his Junior Thesis for his AP History class, and his hard work throughout high school pulling up B's to B+'s for GPA sake. The extra help he sought out for math to get that A on the term test was not as important as the solid contact of the barrel of his bat with an 88 mile per hour fastball in front of the college scouts in attendance.

National Letter of Intent Day was November 9, and on November 8 an envelope arrived from an overnight service—Sam's commitment letter from Boston College. Nothing informal about this sucker. There were three copies of the letter of intent and three copies of BC's scholarship commitment to Sam, citing his "agreement to enroll in the Fall of 2006." Underscored in bold type was the line, "Do not sign these documents prior to 7:00 A.M. on the National Letter of Intent signing date."

Seated at the kitchen island on Wednesday, November 9, at exactly 7:00 A.M., Sam signed the letter while his mom snapped a picture. A couple of days later, there was a press conference at North when a couple of Sam's high-profile classmates signed letters to play Division I basketball at two of the better hoop institutions in the land. Senior guards Anthony Gurley and Corey Lowe sat in front of cameras and microphones and scratched their names as their coach explained that each player was receiving an award worth something in the neighborhood of $200,000. Gurley, a six foot three guard (he, too, had a key to our house and a toothbrush in the second-floor bathroom), was going to

Wake Forest. Lowe was bound for Providence. No one could remember two guards from the same Massachusetts high school
getting scholarships to Division I colleges in the same year. Small
wonder the basketball Tigers were preparing to defend a state
championship.

During these dark-early days of November, Sam was talking
about not playing basketball for the upcoming season. It was a
crushing prospect for his needy dad, but there was no way to
influence my son on this matter. He was 18. He had a baseball
scholarship. He was holding up his end. He even stacked a cord
of apple wood that was dumped in our driveway. He'd played
eleven years of organized basketball—many of them with Messrs.
Gurley and Lowe—and we'd all seen the game pass him by. He
was a five foot ten wannabe power forward on a team with stud
guards who measured six foot three and two. He was a baseball player in a football body with none of the standard physical skills needed for basketball. He wasn't tall and had no outside shot. And yet the idea of Sam hanging up his sneakers was
appalling to me. Sam had endured the humbling junior year on
junior varsity. He'd learned how to play the game correctly. And
now he was going to retire a year early—when he had a chance
to ride the bench for the potential two-time state champs? All
I could do was point out the obvious benefits of playing—foot
speed, camaraderie, a last go-around with kids he'd been playing
with for more than a decade—and hope he decided to try out
for the team.

He missed the official basketball meeting, a telling gesture
and an insult that the varsity coach would not be able to forgive.
Compounding the sin, he scribbled potential Newton North batting lineups on the back of the basketball application envelope.

"Is that ironic?" Sam wondered.

We were always kidding about the misuse of irony. I main-
tained that it was best never to use the word since it was too of-

ten substituted for coincidence (Alanis Morrisette's song "Isn't It Ironic?" cites multiple examples of things that are patently not ironic), but Sam liked to probe the proper use of the mysterious word. It struck him as ironic that he'd be writing baseball line-ups on the envelope that housed his basketball application.

I told him my favorite "ironic" story, a small-town tale involving a bat and ball, naturally.

Like a lot of baseball lifers, my boyhood chum John Iannacci wanted to keep hitting, fielding, and throwing after high school. If you are not a college-caliber player, and you live in central Massachusetts, your best option tends to be softball. After graduating from college, John got married, had a couple of kids, and built his own home on an apple farm in Lunenburg, Massachusetts. He prolonged his life on the diamond, serving as player-manager of a modified fast-pitch team populated with some high school teammates, plus a brother-in-law and friends from work. The league featured teams sponsored by local farms and businesses—even an entry from the correctional institute in Shirley. Every year, it seemed, John's boys would cop the regular-season title, earning home field advantage for the playoffs, only to be foiled by injuries, bad calls, or bum luck. Eventually, they came together for one last season, agreeing that they'd hang up their cleats after one final quest for the grail. They even came up with a curtain-call slogan: "Take no prisoners." You can guess where this is going. John's boys won the regular-season title, advanced to the final round of the playoffs where they were guaranteed to get three out of five at home in the championship round . . . then found themselves up against the prison team in the finals. The hard-earned home field advantage went down the tubes because the correctional team couldn't leave the joint. The Big House provides the ultimate home field advantage. John's boys were pretty upset with this development after all their hard work, but things took a turn in their favor on the eve of the final game, when the star pitcher and catcher of the correctional team escaped. Taking no prisoners, Iannacci's boys finally got their trophy. Truly ironic. I think.

In mid-autumn of '05, Sam was the subject of a full-blown article written by Mike Reiss in the *Globe*'s West Weekly section. At the time, I was engulfed in a messy controversy when a large faction of Red Sox Nation chose to blame me for the resignation of wildly popular Sox general manager, Theo Epstein. Less than twenty-four hours before Theo's bombshell announcement, I'd written a column that represented my take on Theo's relationship with his boss, Sox CEO Larry Lucchino. The story was largely greeted as far too favorable to the unpopular Lucchino at the expense of wunderkind Theo. A shit storm came my way when Theo resigned the next day. The *Globe*'s conflicted relationship with the Sox came into play (the *New York Times,* which owns the *Globe,* owns 17 percent of the ball club), and there was blame and pain throughout our region. Naturally, Sam was oblivious to my travails. He got a kick out of my hate mail but was otherwise unmoved. It is the natural bliss of being 18. We all wish we had it—and the power sleeps (when's the last time you slept past noon?) that come with it.

I went to Los Angeles for a week to appear on ESPN's *Jim Rome Is Burning,* to work on book projects, and to get away from the Theo fallout. While I was gone, Sam procrastinated with his Boston College application. It was almost as if he felt the need to be difficult because the process was going to be so easy for him. Most of his classmates were sweating and filling out multiple (not forty-seven, I hope) applications. I remembered designating our dining room as the War Room when Sarah went about the process of applying to six colleges. So now Sam was showing us that he could still make this difficult even when it was teed up for him.

Marilou indicated that he'd broken up with a girlfriend while

I was away. As far as we knew, this was a first of sorts, primarily because Sam never owned up to having any girlfriends in the first place. There were a lot of girls and a lot of friends but no girlfriends. Marilou worried about the new permissiveness (like we were different?) and "friends with benefits" and a 2005 high school environment in which teens didn't date or go steady as much as they "hook up." I preferred to fall back on the usual "don't ask, don't tell" guy mentality. Sam always hated to talk about sex. I think it embarrassed him more than it embarrassed me to try to talk about it. All kids think they know everything anyway, and I knew he already knew what he needed to know by the time we had "the talk" when we were alone in a hotel on a family road trip when he was about 12. I told him he didn't know as much as he thought he knew and don't be afraid to ask, but I knew he never would. As he entered his teens, every now and then, always in the car (why is it always in the car with dads and sons?), always during daylight, I'd ask, "Got any questions about the sex stuff?" and he would say no and quickly turn up the radio.

He did respond differently once. We were driving around and I'd figured it was time to check in, so I threw out the "Got any questions about the sex stuff?" and he came back with "No. And are you gonna bring this up every time we go to the batting cages? That's always when you bring this up."

I pledged to myself not to do that anymore. It could make a young guy want to stop hitting.

Sam knew the message: "Respect girls the way you'd want guys to respect your sisters. And don't get anybody pregnant."

That was pretty much it. I'm Irish. I didn't want to tell him any more than that, and I really didn't want to think about what he might be up to. I knew it was going to be easier for him than it was for me (he was better-looking, more athletic, more popular, and lived in a more permissive time than his dad), but I also knew that Sam wanted to play baseball in college and he was mindful of things that could foil his plan. This is how I convinced myself that he'd steer clear of booze, drugs, and teen pregnancy. Sam very much liked the "don't ask, don't tell" system. He knew a lot of cute, smart, and funny girls, and he did seem to have respect for them. He and Kate had always been thicker than thieves, and he knew she'd beat him up if he disrespected a nice girl. And until he was about 16, he truly worried that Kate could beat him up. Meanwhile, he'd covered himself with some glory defending the honor of his sister Sarah in the infamous New Year's Eve Bash of 2003 at the Shaughnessy residence.

The whole story of the New Year's Eve Bash has never been told. Personally, I don't want to know all of it. This much I know: in a moment of sheer insanity, Marilou and I decided it would be okay to make a trip to Nantucket to celebrate New Year's Eve in December 2003. At the time, Sarah was two years out of high school, Kate was a freshman at Boston University, and Sam was a sophomore at North. They were all still teenagers, well below drinking age, and there were approximately 2,000 friends of the Shaughnessy teens within a five-mile radius of our house for that holiday season. Given those facts, what responsible parent wouldn't take off for an overnight trip, leaving the house in the custody of three teen siblings?

Like I said, I don't know all that happened, but I do know that when we got home the front door had a broken window and a chair on the porch was splintered. And despite cleanup efforts that no doubt took several hours and numerous trips to CVS for trash bags and air freshener, months later we still were finding plastic cups of beer and wine in the most bizarre places. It was like an archaeological dig of Newton's teen population. Anyway, the only good thing to come of all this was the admission that at some point during the festivities, young Sam used brute force to bounce a misbehaving former boyfriend. I didn't press for details. That was enough.

Which gets us back to Sam and his nongirlfriends. Our favorite always has been tiny Teo, a cute girl who comes over to watch movies and episodes of *Curb Your Enthusiasm.* Teo weighs 100 pounds and crawled into Kate's new suitcase just to show us that she could fit, or maybe to settle a bet. She was born in Bulgaria and gave us a Bulgarian goat bell for our front foyer door (anyone trying to sneak in or out after hours gets busted by the Bulgarian goat bell). Teo never seems to be able to finish a sandwich. One afternoon in our kitchen, I inhaled the last bite of her hamburger and she told me, "In Bulgaria, that means you now know all my secrets." I love to listen to her talk to her mom on her cell phone because she ducks out of the room holding the phone to her ear while speaking Bulgarian. I'm not sure if that means her mom doesn't speak English or she's just keeping secrets from us, but I always say, "You know, Teo, you really don't have to leave the room when you talk to your mom. You could be telling her that we're all fat and ugly and we'd never know."

Kate thinks it's a good thing that Sam and Teo aren't doing the boyfriend-girlfriend thing. Kate's theory is that the high school romances never last, so it's better if Sam and Teo remain "just friends"; this will allow them to connect in a more meaningful way later. Me? I stay quiet about these things. I want to tell him that he'll never find anybody better than this girl, but who wants that kind of advice from their dad when they are 18?

When I spoke to Sam on the phone from California, we both knew I wasn't going to be asking about any girls, but I did check in on the basketball situation. Tryouts were just over a week away. He'd have to decide by then.

"Any more thoughts on basketball?" I asked.

"I don't think so," he said. "We'll talk about it when you get home."

I'm not into forcing a kid to do much of anything, unless it's related to health, SAT prep, or room cleaning, but I was getting close to making a stink about basketball. And I kept wondering why. Was it for him or for me? Always a disturbing question for any parent to ask himself.

Bill Shaughnessy was a sophomore in the autumn of 1962 when Groton had a brand new high school and a brand new basketball coach. I'd seen the school rise from dirt—it was adjacent to the dusty recess yard of our elementary school. My sister Joan had been president of student council and was allowed to stick a shovel in the earth when they broke ground. The new school was pretty impressive, with chemistry labs and a big stage at one end of the cafeteria, but all I knew was that it had the shiniest hardwood basketball court I'd ever seen. Our house was only a short walk from school, and the way my bed was positioned, I could actually see the gym lights at night when my head hit the pillow.

The new coach was a 22-year-old man named John P. Fahey. He was also my gym teacher. He yelled a lot and made us do calisthenics and all the stuff required by President Kennedy's newly created Council on Physical Fitness. You could tell that the big kids believed in this new young guy. Mr. Fahey got the basketball players' attention by cutting a bunch of senior lettermen on the first day of practice. The team had been 0-14 the year before he arrived, and the new coach saw no future in a bunch of senior losers who'd been junior losers and showed up complacent and confident in their senior status. I'm told there was a small outcry by some of the boys' parents (nothing like the town meeting scene in *Hoosiers* when the locals want to get rid of Gene Hackman, but impressive by Groton standards), but it turned out that young Mr. Fahey knew what he was doing. In Fahey's second season, the Groton High Crusaders went 20-0 and won the league championship.

Riding the officials, carrying a towel throughout the game, young Jack Fahey became something of a Groton celebrity. All the dads and other townsfolk admired what he was doing with the boys, and conversations about last night's game were carried on at the counter of Dixon's Drugstore and Bruce's Pharmacy throughout the winter months. All I knew was that I wanted to play for him when I got to high school. In the meantime, Mr. Fahey let me serve as ballboy and ride the bus to road games on Friday nights. Tuesday game nights were deemed too late for me.

I was not a confident young man when I entered high school in 1967. I was still only five foot two and clearly wasn't going to carry on the legacy of brother Bill. In a way it was almost better that I was small and only marginally good at baseball and basketball. It was pretty easy for everyone seeing me to figure out right away that Dan Shaughnessy wasn't going to be another Bill Shaughnessy. It sort of took the pressure off.

But I still wanted to be on the team. One of the great days of my life came in December of my sophomore year when Billy Hamilton came into study hall and said they'd posted the varsity roster in the boy's locker room. I ran downstairs and saw my name on the sheet tacked to the corkboard. I was Mr. Fahey's twelfth man. Thirty-seven years later, I went to a theater in Boston, watched Billy Crystal's magical *700 Sundays*, and almost wept when he got to the part about his high school basketball coach keeping him on the team even though he wasn't very big or very good. The famous actor recalled, "It's the nicest thing anyone's ever done for me."

Sitting in the Opera House, I took out my notebook and wrote that down. And now I'm writing it again. And I realize that Sam has none of this feeling. He's had good coaches in his eleven years of basketball, and he's played with kids far more talented than Bill Shaughnessy. He's got classmates walking around wearing basketball jackets that say "Massachusetts State Champions," kids who are going to play big-time college ball. But so much is different since the days when a high school basketball team could galvanize an entire town. How could Sam know that making the varsity basketball team could change somebody's life?

It changed mine. A few months after riding the pine for the first-place 1968–69 Crusaders, I decided to run for class president. And I won. A year later, I won again. I started asking girls out on dates and sometimes they'd say yes (movies or bowling —that was it—and there were no "benefits," trust me). Making the team gave me identity and confidence. I think it even somehow made me taller. And John P. Fahey has been part of my life ever since. He was a pallbearer when my father died in 1979, and he was with me in the early innings of that cold May day when Sam hit the walkoff against Braintree.

So the answer was yes. I was projecting myself, my story, on Sam's basketball decision. Tryouts weren't scheduled until the Monday after Thanksgiving, so we dropped the topic for a while. Basketball was the sport that must not be named.

Thanksgiving morning featured the 111th playing of the annual turkey day football game between Newton and Brookline. Brookline is perhaps best known as the birthplace of John. F. Kennedy. Like Newton, it's full of college graduates, authors, Volvos, and flaming liberals. It's the People's Republic of Brookline. Brookline High School alums include Mike Wallace, Michael Dukakis, Patriot owner Robert Kraft, and Theo Epstein. Lately Newton's been having its way with the Warriors, but going into Thanksgiving 2005 the series was deadlocked, 52-52-6. Still, it did not figure to be a rough game for Newton. Our team was 8-2, bound for the playoffs, while Brookline staggered into late November with an 0-10 record.

High school football on Thanksgiving is a Massachusetts tradition, and it was only recently that I learned it's not part of the high school experience in most states of the Union. Scholastic playoff games in Texas draw 40,000 fans. In the Commonwealth, we watch our boys get together at 10 A.M., while twenty-five-pound turkeys are roasting in ovens across the state. The annual Thanksgiving game offers college freshmen the first opportunity to see the kids they went to school with for twelve years. They're easy to spot. They gather at one end of the field, wearing their new school colors, exchanging stories about freshman year, and paying absolutely no attention to the twenty-two boys smashing helmets on the field. When the clock runs out, there is an onslaught of hugs and phony promises of hanging out over the short break.

Newton beat Brookline on Thanksgiving 39–0. Another good day for the class of '06.

During the holiday weekend, Sam asked his mom if our neighbor, Joe Inskeep, a Buddhist minister, would mind talking to him about Buddhism. Marilou was thrilled. I was apprehensive. We knew that Joe would be only too happy to instruct Sam on the mysteries of another religion, and it was somewhat remarkable that Sam (born the same day as Gandhi, whatever that's worth) was interested in anything other than baseball bats.

I grew up in a strict Catholic household. My parents took us to church every Sunday and Mom sprinkled holy water on our heads any time there was threat of a thunderstorm. My sister Ann was not allowed to attend a baby shower for a classmate who got pregnant in high school. Sins were not to be celebrated and Catholic dogma was not to be challenged. The priest was always right. At the age of 10, I was brought to the local convent (Sisters of the Sacred Heart) and my parents told the nuns, "Danny wants to be an altar boy." I don't remember having any say in the matter. Next thing I knew, I was learning the Latin responses that needed to be recited from the altar. It turned out I was one of the last kids in America to undergo such instruction. About a half hour after I learned the Latin Mass, American Catholics switched to English. My dad, who went to Catholic schools his entire life and counted the collection money on Sundays, was dismayed. I was delighted.

I served Mass every week until my sophomore year of high school. Lent was our playoff season, and Holy Week was the Series. During Communion, I was assigned to hold the golden plate under the chins of all the communicants. The plate assured that all potential host dust would be captured when the priest made the transfer from chalice to the mouths of our parishioners. And in the event of a dropped host, I'd be there to catch the body and blood of Christ—like a net under a trapeze act. One day, while I was simultaneously holding the plate, counting the house, and looking around for high school cuties, Father Carroll actually dropped the host while he was making the transfer . . . *and I did not catch it with my plate!*

Unbelievable. Five years of standing at the altar like a doofus, holding the stupid plate in case of an error, and the one time the priest dropped the host, I failed to make the catch. In 1966, a host on the carpet was no laughing matter. Father Carroll secured the area, making everyone stand back while he went to his knees to retrieve the Holy Eucharist. He couldn't have embarrassed me more if he'd cordoned off the area with police tape.

I never gulped the altar wine. It smelled like vinegar. As for unwanted sexual advances by priests, there were none. Maybe I was too naive to know, but none of the holy men ever hit on me. Not even later in my four years at Holy Cross. For the most part, priests were some of the finest men I knew.

My dad certainly felt that way, and he'd have popped a blood vessel if one of his kids ever wanted to explore Buddhism. We weren't even allowed to go into Protestant churches in Groton. It was different for Sam. This was 2005, and we lived in Newton, where anything goes and independent thinking is celebrated. Marilou supplied Sam with a small library on Buddhism and he ploughed through the material as if it were a baseball bat catalogue. My son, the Buddhist.

December

THE BASKETBALL DILEMMA went down to the wire, and now that it's over I can say I'm not proud of my part in the episode.

While Sam was saying he did not want to go out for the team, I reminded him of the obvious advantages. He could be with his friends, working out every afternoon, and there would be a lot of sweet victories, maybe even a return trip to the Boston Garden. He'd invested eleven winters of his life playing hoops with the same guys who were now ranked number 47 in the country by *Sports Illustrated*. He'd gotten up early for the Saturday practices and learned how to play the game correctly. He knew how to pass, run the floor, box out, and defend.

"I hate basketball," Sam would say at the end of these discussions.

And then I'd go back and recite all the reasons he should play. Deep down, I knew I wanted to see him on that Boston Garden floor, if only for warm-ups. So I'd ask him if this wasn't some kind of defense mechanism. Was he afraid he'd be cut if he tried out? Was that it? The coach had told me a year earlier that he was counting on Sam to be one of his senior leaders, a presence at practice, and a good team guy. Sam had done the hard time of playing junior varsity as a junior. Why do that if not for a senior season on the bench with the state champs? It made no sense.

"I hate basketball."

I couldn't hear that because I remembered the best nights of my high school life, when the winter wind would whip around the steeples and silos and the high school gym was full of friends, neighbors, and sweet sweat. Parents and townsfolk gathered in the back row of the Groton High bleachers, and we felt like big men in our little town. When our games were over, we'd walk to our cars with our just-showered hair crystallizing into ice under an infinite black sky. Cheerleaders, still in their burgundy uniforms, would ride with us to the pizza place over in Ayer, and we'd tell basketball stories that we still sometimes recite: the now boring stories of glory days.

Sam was allegedly still deliberating on the weekend before tryouts. In fact, he had already made up his mind but was still trying to figure out a way to appease his dad. He was also dealing with a parentally imposed deadline for his Boston College application. Frustrated by the normal procrastination of the 3-2 kid, Marilou threw up her hands and put me in charge. It was quite silly, really. Sam's BC application was a bag job—no different from that of any other recruited athlete who'd already been okayed by admissions. There was no suspense about it, none of the apprehension that was so much a part of the process for his older sisters. Still, Sam seemed to be having trouble finishing the job, which involved little more than postage. Ever the enabler, I dug into the bottom of my desk drawer and found a sleeve with some sheets of dusty Elvis stamps. They were made in 1993, when a stamp cost only 29 cents, and I'd given them to Sarah for her application to Harvard back in 2002. Who in admissions could resist checking out the application of any kid who applied under the cover of the King?

Smiling at the sight of the old stamps, Sam slapped four of

them on his BC application, and we got in the car to drive to the mailbox for the ceremonial drop. Mission accomplished, Sam got back behind the wheel and drove . . . to the mall. He said nothing.

This was a ride not unlike the one we made to Boston College back in October, when we didn't know whether he'd decided on BC or Notre Dame. This time, Sam led me into the Foot Locker at Watertown's Arsenal Mall.

Still silent, he started trying on basketball shoes. He found a pair of size 13 Nikes that worked, and the salesman—wearing a referee shirt—went to ring up the purchase. I stopped Sam before we got the counter and said, "One last chance, big guy. I don't want you twenty years from now telling me that Dad made you play basketball against your wishes. We can stop now if you want. It's not too late."

He just smiled and nodded and said, "I want to play."

Everything was different the next night when I got home from work and Sam was sitting at the island in our kitchen, eating a plate of meat, and shaking his head. He said he had no chance to make the team. "The coach hates me," he said. He said the coach had him working out with sophomores on the fifth string. Sam further endeared himself to the staff when one of his hard passes hit Anthony Gurley smack in the face.

I said he needed to talk to the coach, one on one. He needed to ask, "What do I have to do to make this team?" He needed to find out if he had a fair shot. Give it a week, I told him. Don't let the guy make you quit.

I had trouble sleeping that night. I kept rolling over, thinking about Sam and basketball. It reminded me of three years earlier when I tossed and turned while pondering Sarah's prospects for admission to the schools of her choice. It was the same when Kate was frustrated by her role on the volleyball team, fearful of the wrath of her coach. After about an hour of thrashing in the sheets, I wondered, What do people who don't have kids worry about at night? Why is this so important to me? Is Sam losing any sleep over this?

My father never did this. *You trying out for basketball? Good. See you in March when they hand out the letter sweaters—that is, if I'm not working that night.*

Larry Bird once told me a story about how little his dad cared about his high school basketball career. The gym wasn't far from the Bird household, but Bird senior wasn't always motivated to make the short walk. One night Larry's uncle had to call his dad at halftime to tell him to come down to the gym because his son was about to set some kind of scoring record. These were not camcorder parents.

Why are we so much more involved with the ups and downs of our children's lives than our parents were? Is it because we have the time? Is it because we aren't worried about paying the fuel bill? We certainly don't love our kids any more than our parents loved us. Why were they able to let us figure it out for ourselves, when we are so intent on being involved every step of the way? Why are we such enablers and what kind of a dependent generation are we raising? It seems as if today's parents take on the roles traditionally assigned to grandparents—forget the tough love and just give the kid whatever he wants.

When I was a teenager, parents were parents and kids were kids and they pretty much stayed out of each other's way. Our parents were simply not involved in the day-to-day operations of our after-school activities. Attendance at our ball games was neither required nor expected. Mom and Dad often did not know the name of our coach during a given season. When my parents did attend our baseball games, they would usually park their Ford Galaxie on top of a hill way down the left field line and occasionally toot the horn if something good happened. I'm told Dad did a bit of bragging about brother Bill's accomplishments, but he'd never have done that in front of us, because it would have emphasized athletics over academics and he certainly didn't want me to feel badly because I was not as good a ballplayer as my older brother.

Today we are a nation of grownups who raise children like thoroughbred horses, micromanaging every aspect of a child's life and making sure that the kid attains all accolades and awards that eluded the parent. It used to be "My son made honor roll" on a bumper sticker; now parents put banners on the side of their homes exclaiming, "Suzie made cheerleader captain!" I've heard of parents who attended high school sports team *practices,* just to see how things are going.

Deep down, I wanted to be at basketball practice to see if Sam was fairly characterizing his plight, but I got hold of my senses and dismissed the crazy notion.

When I came home after the second day of basketball practice, Sam was on the couch, watching TV. He said he'd talked with the coach. He said he twice asked what he had to do to make the team, and both times the coach said he couldn't answer the question. According to Sam, he had no chance to make this team. I told him it sounded like the coach was afraid to cut him because he'd done the time as a junior on JV and it would strike people as unfair. Other kids who had quit as juniors were being offered a chance to play. It looked to me as if the coach wanted Sam to quit so he wouldn't have to cut him. I asked Sam how he'd feel if I talked to the coach.

"No," he said. "You talking to him is not like any other parent talking to him. If you talk to him and he keeps me, I'll be uncomfortable with that."

So there it was. A lesson learned. This was stupid. I was being the kind of parent I hate. I was imposing my wishes on my son to make myself feel better. This was about me, not Sam, and I needed to move on.

Frustrated, I told him, "Do whatever you want. The guy wants you to quit. You'll be making it easy for him, and he can always say that you didn't want to play basketball in the first place. I'd rather see you make it hard for him and make him cut you. It's only another week out of your life. But I'm done talking about it."

Sam quit the next day. Wednesday. I had to cover a Celtics game that night and didn't see him. We spoke only briefly on the phone.

"Sam asked me if you are mad at him," Marilou said early Thursday.

When he got home late that afternoon, he asked me if I wanted to go in the hot tub. Good idea. Great thoughts have been exchanged in the hot tub. Much like the golf course or the steam room at a health club, where captains of industry broker mergers. Much like the drive to the dump in Groton back in the day.

My son was being unusually solicitous and tentative.

"Watch out for the rock," he warned, as I stepped past a boulder we use to keep the tub lid from blowing open during storms.

Very un-Samlike, I thought to myself. He's really feeling guilty about this.

The moment was good and bad. The good part was that I knew Sam was grateful for all we had done for him and that he wanted to please us. He wasn't quite as selfish as I'd feared. It actually bothered him to see that he'd disappointed me. I knew this would be a moment when I could actually get him to move a cord of wood, or clean his room, or drive his sister back to school without getting any backtalk. At that moment, I could have asked him to paint the house over the weekend and he would have readily agreed. But I was also ashamed. I'd done what I said I would never do. I'd made this about me. I'd made him feel badly because he didn't do something that he now sincerely seemed to hate.

Certainly there are times when a son or daughter should carry some guilt for disappointing a parent. Flunking out of school, getting arrested, or burning down the house while hosting a keg party might fall into this category. But dropping out of a sport should be the kid's choice. And I was embarrassed that Sam was upset because of something that was my problem, not his.

"Sam, you know how I feel about this," I said. "I'm disappointed, but it's your life, not mine. In this area, you should do the things you want to do, not the things I want you to do. My feelings really don't matter on this one, and we don't need to talk about it anymore."

Still tentative, still aiming to please and appease, Sam mentioned that he'd gone out for the track team. He said it would help him with baseball and indicated that the practices were more fun and he enjoyed the other kids on the team. I asked him what he planned on trying. It was difficult to imagine a five foot ten, 190-pound sprinter. He said he was running the 400 meters and would try the shot put. I told him it sounded like an okay idea. There wasn't much left to say. Basketball was over.

These were heady days in Newton. Our town was voted safest city in America again, and the North football team made it all the way to the Super Bowl in Rocky Marciano Stadium in Brockton.

With the high school football playoffs in full bloom, there was the usual handwringing about the SAT test being held on the same day as the high school Super Bowls. None of our kids were affected because the Newton game wasn't scheduled to start until 4 P.M., but some players at other schools faced the dilemma of choosing between the SATs and the Super Bowl. I would not have wanted to make this choice had any of my kids been involved. There's always another SAT test. A Super Bowl is a once-in-a-lifetime decision.

Sam had one final test to take to fulfill his BC requirements. He'd already knocked off the math requirement, and Marilou bought him a three-hundred-page book to prepare him for the SAT-II literature test. The day before the exam, I found a Sam-note in the kitchen that read, "Mother, I think I'm going to take US History because I did the practice questions online and knew a solid chunk of them. And I thumbed through this (literature) book and felt retarded. Sorry. Your son, Sam (the book's un-touched, returnable)."

The day of the SATs and high school Super Bowls was cold and windy. Sam and I drove to Brockton to see his classmates play Woburn in the MIAA Division 1-A final. I'd offered to cover the game for the *Globe* only because the paper likes to have col-umnists at high school games on occasion, and it was a way to combine work and pleasure. Sam's former freshman coach, the redoubtable Giusti, was on the sideline in his khaki shorts. It was somehow comforting to see his bare legs in the brutal cold wind of Rocky Marciano Stadium in the first week of December.

Despite Giusti's inspiration, the senior leadership, and a high-flying offense that scored 317 points in twelve games, the Tigers were no match for Woburn's Tanners on this day. Wo-burn had a senior running back named Tommy Hart who shred-ded the Newton defense, running for over two hundred yards in a 34–7 blowout win. I was in the press box, hoping to write about the Newton boys, but Woburn owned the day and I was forced to praise the Tanners instead. I'd become acquainted with their veteran coach, Rocky Nelson, because both of our daugh-ters are cancer survivors and we'd been involved in a couple of fundraisers together. This was Rocky's thirty-sixth year at Wo-burn and his twentieth as head coach; he'd never won the big one and I was happy that he finally did. The Tanners had been without a home field during school construction; for a couple of years, those folks drove fifty-five miles to Brockton after a kickoff breakfast at the Tanner saloon. It was all good . . . except for one thing.

Rocky ran up the score. Leading 27–7 with three minutes to play, the Tanners took over on the Newton 35-yard line and kept pounding, scoring another touchdown. I wanted to write a column about sportsmanship and the meaning of high school athletics, but this wasn't the time. It was more important to let Woburn have their day. I didn't have the heart to say anything to Rocky about it when he was surrounded by joyous family members after the game. But I wanted to ask him why he went for the last touchdown and why his starters were still in the game when he could have emptied the bench and allowed another ten kids to someday say they played in a Super Bowl victory at Rocky Marciano Stadium.

Newton's head coach, the English teacher Peter Capidulipo, a veteran of twenty-two years, said all the right things in defeat. He talked about how tough it would be for the kids because we tend to remember how things end, and he didn't want this blowout defeat to be their memory of the season. "I hope after some time goes by that they'll be able to look at the whole season and all the good things they did in their four years here," he said.

We got a card in the mail from Boston College indicating that they had everything they needed regarding Sam's application and that he would be hearing from them in April. It reminded me that we probably needed to light a fire under the other high school senior sleeping regularly on our second floor, Alexis Mongo.

Alexis has been part of our family for thirteen years. Sam and Alexis met on the day before the first day of kindergarten at the Underwood Elementary School, and when school officials solicited Newton parents to sign on as Metco host parents, Marilou raised her hand and we had another kid, part-time, for more than a decade. The Metco program offers suburban educations to a few of Boston's city children. It's been somewhat controversial over the years because it inflates the city tax base, and there can be resentment when/if Metco kids take team spots that could have gone to kids from Newton, or Wellesley, or any other town involved in the sports program. Woe to the seventh grade basketball coach who keeps five Metco kids and cuts seven sons of Newton taxpayers.

Not every Metco kid has a host family, but it's a bonus because these young people endure long days with tedious commutes. They get up at least an hour earlier than their schoolmates, and if they're involved in an after-school activity, they face a fourteen-hour day. Bringing Alexis into our home made life easier for Alexis and his mom, who was in her early twenties when we first gave him a bed. It also gave Sam a sense of what it's like to have a brother.

Alexis's mom, Raquel, is Puerto Rican and his dad, Thomas, is half black and half Portuguese. When his hair is appropriately cornrowed, Alexis looks a little like rapper/actor Ludacris, and more than once opposing fans chanted "Luda" when he was on the basketball court for Newton North. His parents were already split when we first met him, and he has a younger sister, Paris. Living in the city and putting two kids through Newton schools while navigating the red tape of Metco has been exhausting and confusing for Raquel. Doing it as a single mom only made things that much tougher, and we've been blessed to have Alexis as part of our autumns, winters, and springs during Sam's school years.

When I thumb through snapshots of Sam's youth, Alexis is always there. Attending birthday parties, playing soccer, eating Happy Meals, graduating elementary school, playing street basketball, trick-or-treating, eating at the island counter in our kitchen, holding football helmets after a junior high game, graduating middle school, shoveling snow, stacking cordwood, taking out the trash, needing rides to SAT practice . . . he's been there every step of the way. I remember the day he cut his ear when he fell on a rusty milk crate on the front porch and had to go to the hospital. I remember earlier this year when we got up on a Saturday morning and took him to get his driver's license. We picked up celebratory doughnuts on the way home.

We worked on his college essay just before Christmas.

"Sometimes people judge me on my appearance," he wrote. "But I refuse to be what they want me to be—just some ethnic kid from the ghetto in baggy clothes. What you see is not what you get with me. A lot of people judge me first just as a jock from a rough city neighborhood, but there are many dimensions to my personality. The Real Me: the athlete, the student, the brother, the son."

The essay didn't need much work.

How to gauge Alexis's influence on our household through the years? Sam came to rap music at a fairly early age, but given the pop culture of most suburban schools in the northeast, that probably would have happened anyway. Sarah and Kate have always teased Sam about his choice of music and clothing, and the popular phrase hurled his way was "Sam, you're not black!" which generated a few good laughs.

As a man who grew up in a land of white birches and white folks, I've learned much from having Alexis in our home through the years. Groton was too white. Boston is too white. Our kids are better for growing up in a time when color doesn't seem to matter as much. Like homosexuality and gay marriage, race seems to be an issue for parents more than kids.

A couple of years ago, I went back to my old high school and watched a basketball triple-header between the towns of Groton and Lunenburg. Midway through the varsity joust, after watching the freshmen and junior varsity games, I realized that I hadn't seen more than one or two minorities all day long. That was including parents, cheerleaders, coaches, and players. Forty years after I grew up, the small towns in central Massachusetts were still a whiter shade of pale. Maybe even whiter than before.

There were three black families in Groton when I grew up. The Hamiltons. The Hazards. And the Gaskins. I knew the Hamiltons best. Mr. Hamilton worked at the hardware store and marched in the Memorial Day parade with my father. Billy Hamilton was a year ahead of me in school and a pretty fair hitter in Little League. We call him "Big Hams," and he still lives near Groton.

When I was still in high school, I remember my older sister Mary being amazed when she came to the house and Big Hams was hanging out with me and several other friends. Her experience as a teen had been completely different. Mary went to the University of New Hampshire in the fall of 1960, and her first roommate was black. I did not know about any of this until much later, but it turns out my parents didn't want her to bring her roommate to our home for a weekend. The times they were a-changin', but not yet in Groton, Massachusetts. This was 1960, and my folks were afraid of what other people might think. To this day I am amazed, because my father served in World War II and was a God-fearing man who worked for the church and seemed to look out for the disenfranchised in his supervisory position at the local paper factory. An entry in my high school diary, from August 1969, reports an exchange between me and a black man who came to the ice cream stand. My dad had given the man some extra tires we had in our garage, and I wrote, "That fat negro man that Dad gave the tires to came down to Johnson's. He's nice. He said, 'You got a good old man there.' That made me so proud of Dad."

Weird that I was still using the word *Negro*, but more telling is the realization that in the seven hundred daily entries over my junior and senior years of high school, this is one of the few times I said anything complimentary about either one of my parents. I was annoyed at their ceaseless questions about how my day had gone. Most of my diary writings are about girls I was trying to date (with little success), our basketball and baseball teams, and the state of my complexion and hair. But clearly, something in the man's message moved me on that hot Thursday afternoon. A black man had said something nice about the generosity and character of my father and it meant something. This is why it's still difficult to account for my parents' backward thinking in 1960. I have no answers, but clearly my folks were far more enlightened by the time their fifth child was ready for college, and there never again was an issue about who was allowed, or not allowed, in our home.

Still, my parents were the whitest people I ever knew. In the early 1970s, when I was home from college in the springtime, I met Steve Hazard at the town field, and we spent the early evening playing basketball until it got dark. I gave Steve a ride home that night in Mom's tan Buick Riviera and didn't think about it again until my next encounter with Steve, when he asked if he'd left his comb in my mom's car. These were the days of the Angela Davis Afros, and Steve's comb was more weapon than grooming device. I knew there was no way my parents would have been able to identify such an item, but that didn't mean they didn't have it. When I got home I asked the folks if they'd seen Steve's comb. I explained that it was a large object with a wooden handle and long steel prongs.

Sounding not unlike Edith Bunker, my mother put her hand to her face and said, "Oh, is *that* what that is?"

Mom went to the green kitchen cabinet above the sink, opened the door, and removed Steve's comb from the shelf.

"I thought this was a cheese cutter," she said.

Made sense. Who could hold this thing in their hand without wanting to drop it down over a log of Cracker Barrel?

Next time I saw Steve, I presented him with the comb and said, "Haz, you're not going to believe it, but my mom thought this thing was a cheese cutter."

"She cut any cheese with it?" he asked quickly.

I told him no. But the truth has never been learned.

Steve was three years behind me in school and his later high school experience, and maybe a good part of his life after school, was shaped by an unfortunate event in a basketball game when he was a junior. The Groton team was on the verge of winning the league championship in the closing moments of a home game against Quabbin Regional High School. Groton was set to wrap things up when Steve lost track of the score and intentionally fouled a player from Quabbin, thinking Groton needed to get the ball back. Naturally, the Quabbin kid made the free throws, Groton lost the championship, and Steve was the goat. He was one of the most promising players in the school—a junior playing in crunch time of a big game—but he quit basketball after that season. According to guys who played on the team, Steve was never the same kid in the years that followed. He never stopped blaming himself, and he wouldn't let his friends talk him out of it.

Just about the time Alexis was putting his applications in the mail, more news broke from the political correctness front. Principal Huntington announced an end to official graduation program tradition of putting asterisks next to the names of students who had achieved academic excellence.

"I wonder who first objected to that?" Marilou asked aloud, to no one in particular.

"Someone whose kid *sucks* at everything," snapped Kate.

"Everyone comes in as a class and graduates as a class," said the principal. "I love the fact that at graduation I look out at the sea of black caps and gowns and know that everybody gets exactly the same diploma."

The school paper editorial chimed in: "We see graduation as a time for students to be together and celebrate completion of four years of hard work. It is not a time for division."

Groan. Once again, we don't want to hurt anyone's feelings and once again we celebrate sameness rather than reward individual achievement. We did it when they were 6 and we made sure they all got trophies even if they didn't win a game. We did it when they played soccer and we didn't keep score so that nobody would feel badly. We did it with the tug of peace instead of the tug of war. And now we're going to do it at graduation. We're going to make sure that the kids with the straight A's don't get recognized at the expense of others perhaps less gifted, perhaps less hard-working. Why on earth would an institution of learning want to recognize academic achievement?

"It's the same in everything at North," Kate reminded me. "No prom queens. No valedictorians. At North, we're all prom queens and valedictorians."

And now they'll all graduate without recognition of academic honors.

January

MARILOU WOKE UP in a sweat one night and said she'd dreamed that Sam got busted for possession of marijuana. I told her that there was a greater likelihood he'd be spotted buying a ticket to *Guys and Dolls.* In other words, forget about it and go back to sleep.

Sam was nine months' shy of college, and that meant we were still allowed to worry about doomsday scenarios. This vanishes when they finish high school. Kids go off to college and we have no idea how late they are out, who they are with, or what they might be up to. But as long as a child is still under our roof, living in the high school universe, house rules apply and we worry about anything that might blow up the plan. Years earlier, the son of one of our neighbors jeopardized his college admission when he got arrested at a high school pot party. More recently, we'd come to learn that one of Sam's high school friends, a kid who'd crashed in Sam's room more than once, was busted by his own mom. The young man was caught with marijuana, which he intended to sell. There's nothing particularly revolutionary about any of this, but it speaks to the sensitive nature of these final, fragile days of young people living in our home.

Our second floor Teenage Wasteland was in sorry shape after the holidays. Sam's sisters were both home on break, and we also had Kate's boyfriend (his parents live in California), Alexis, and random high school seniors grabbing some floor when both beds in Sam's room were occupied. I had missed all this chaos when the girls were away, and it reminded me of how quiet it was going to be for most of the rest of our days here after Sam graduates. Not something I'm looking forward to. I think I'll leave the second floor bathroom light on as a household eternal flame.

Louisville Sluggers littered the bedrooms throughout the house, mingling with dirty laundry and boxes of opened Christmas gifts (I gave Sam my dad's Boston College '36 ring). At a neighborhood New Year's party, Cheryl, a mother of five from across the street, told me, "I see Sam through the window at night, swinging his baseball bat."

Something else I was going to miss.

I like the chaos of young people home from college—even the noise at 2:30 in the morning when somebody gets up off the sofa, decides to make a baloney sandwich, and yells, "Hey, who wants a sandwich?" Bringing the dorm life to our home, they stay up till 3 A.M., watching reruns of *Sex and the City,* then sleep till after noon. In 1973, when I was a sophomore at college, I came home for a weekend, went to bed Friday night, and slept until 2 o'clock the next afternoon. When I came down the stairs, my dad, sitting in his brown chair, said, "I guess you were tired. It's two in the afternoon." I was stunned. I'd been planning on watching a college basketball game that apparently was already nearing halftime. Then my dad added, "Not only is it two in the afternoon, it's *Sunday!*"

For a second, he had me. I thought maybe I really had slept for a day and a half. But no. My game was on the TV. In progress. It was Saturday. *Good one, Dad.*

There were fourteen books in the "Buddha bin" next to Sam's bed. We hadn't talked much about it. Seems private. But this young man who hated to read immersed himself in *The Lost*

Art of Compassion, Dr. Lorne Ladner's tome on "discovering the practice of happiness in the meeting of Buddhism and Psychology." The bin included *Awakening the Mind, Lightening the Heart* by the Dalai Lama and *Thoughts Without a Thinker* with a foreword by His Holiness.

My theory was that Sam was turning to Tibetan Buddhist teachings to train himself not to overreact when he got called out on strikes in his first at-bat of a game. Skill and talent aside, athletic performance almost always relies heavily on psychological toughness. Look at professional golfers. To a man, they'll tell you that the game is largely mental. In any sport, a confident player with a clear head will perform better. He who dwells on past failures or fears future calamity is destined to fail, especially if he's trying to hit an eighty-mile-per-hour changeup when he's looking for a ninety-mile-per-hour fastball.

This sudden interest in Buddhism didn't stop some of the nonsense in Sam's 18-year-old world. His economics teacher called to tell us that Sam was too much of a class clown. She said he was doing well in class but too often distracted other students with nonstop commentary (a side of Sam we never saw at home) and attempted to make a joke out of everything. He also was discovered sporting a T-shirt that read, "We put the fun in funnel." Apparently, an enterprising senior was selling the shirts to members of the class of '06, and you didn't have to be very hip to find the obvious objectionable element of the message (a funnel and hose apparatus is a standard tool of binge beer drinking on college campuses).

Principal Huntington instructed parents and teachers to take the shirts off the backs of the seniors.

The principal's edict led to the predictable editorial in the student paper, which held "Free speech is crucial for all students. It is the free speech law that prevents the school from stopping Animal Rights Club protests and telling editors of this newspaper what to publish. And it is this law that allows seniors, however inappropriately, to wear shirts saying, 'We put the fun in funnel.'"

I remember those days of righteous indignation. Slogans, too. The Groton High School class of '71 numbered only ninety-one at graduation, and I don't think any of my classmates would argue that ours was perhaps the most listless and unaccomplished group in the history of the school. We had few scholars and athletes. By and large, we were outside the cool loop. We had a lot of long-haired kids experimenting with marijuana and beer, and experiencing the agonizing reappraisal of all young people who came of age in the 1960s and watched Woodstock, Kent State, and Vietnam unfold on our black-and-white television screens. Not particularly active or accomplished, we were thoughtful. Our big contribution to the school was converting the cold war relic/civil defense bomb shelter into a senior lounge where we could smoke without fear of getting caught. I am not kidding. In 1970, the time was ripe to do away with the nuclear hysteria that had traumatized our first- and second-grade years (I remember gathering my favorite teddy bears, baseball cards, and toy soldiers and putting them in a cardboard box during the Cuban missile crisis). In retrospect, it does not seem remarkable that parents and faculty were willing to give up the concrete-enclosed space opposite the boys' locker room, where intrepid Mr. Belitsky had stocked tons of water jugs and dried foods. What is amazing, however, is that they allowed us to convert the area into a dark den with little supervision. In our new clubhouse, boys wore flared pants, girls wore micro-miniskirts, and we listened to the latest work of Crosby, Stills, Nash & Young. Smoking was not sanctioned, but I don't remember any teachers bursting into the dark, hazy shelter. Our senior lounge. Power to the people. Right on.

As president of the class of 1971 (truly, only one other kid ran, and he was from Georgia, which made him the ultimate carpetbagger in a town with no outsiders), I presided over a number of class meetings that gave me a small sense of what it felt like for those assigned to teach us on a daily basis. It could not have been easy, and more than once a veteran teacher told us, "You are the most apathetic bunch of kids I've ever had here."

Our response: "Who cares?"

And there was born the unofficial motto of the Groton High School class of 1971: "Who cares if we're apathetic?"

We thought it was pretty clever and, in retrospect, it's not bad. I have never heard of another motto like it, and we owed the slogan to one of our most talented, iconoclastic classmates, Allan "Albane" Friedrich.

We didn't know much about Albane until the ninth grade because he went to Catholic school until then, so it was quite a big deal when he showed up on the first day of our freshman year of high school. All we knew about him was that he was a rugged kid, a good baseball player, and he had a bunch of sisters with blond hair and spectacular figures. As for his nickname, "Albane," as far as anyone could tell, he'd given it to himself. Albane was an operator. In September 1967, 14-year-old Allen Friedrich was president and CEO of Albanian Enterprises, a multifaceted conglomerate specializing in homemade booze and term papers passed down by older siblings. It was a precursor to the young "enterprising" kids in *Risky Business.*

Dandelion wine was the beverage of choice when Albane first game to Groton High, and he was selling the homemade vintage out of his locker for a couple of years before he got the attention of our principal, Mr. Lewis Karabatsos.

Albane's version of his meeting with the principal went like this:

> Mr. K: Allen, is there any activity you've been up to in school that you think you maybe should tell me about?
> Albane: No.

Mr. K: Well, then, can I order a gallon of that stuff you'd been selling to the students?

That pretty much closed down the alcoholic beverage arm of Albanian Enterprises.

Selling homemade wine back in the day seemed pretty harmless. Almost amusing. But of course, it wasn't. And it isn't. Kids die when they drink and drive. Check the local newspapers over the course of any nine-month school year and invariably you'll come across a photo of a high school cheerleader with perfect teeth who wrapped her birthday-gift sports car around a utility pole after guzzling vodka with other kids at somebody's house. Drinking and driving is certainly not the sole province of high school students, but their tragic endings tend to get more exploitive play on the nightly news. There were plenty of these sad stories in our local papers during the 2005–2006 school year, and we dutifully put them in front of Sam as he sat at the kitchen island, scarfing his meaty dinner fare. We reminded him that this could happen to anyone—good kids die because of one bad mistake. We told him to be careful about decisions, especially late at nights on weekends. Don't get in a car with anyone who's been drinking. Don't be at a party where there's drinking. One bad decision can mess up your entire life, not to mention your precious college baseball plan at Boston College.

In the middle of the month, we all flew to Raleigh, North Carolina, for the wedding of our niece, Katie. Our hotel in Raleigh was entirely nonsmoking, and in our never-ending quest for true examples of irony, Sam and I decided that a no-smoking hotel in the middle of Tobacco Road would probably qualify.

The highlight of the wedding was the presence of Dean Smith, the second most famous resident of North Carolina. Michael Jordan, naturally, can claim to be the most famous living person in state history (Presidents Jackson, Polk, and Andrew

Johnson would make the top five if we expanded the category to include the deceased), but Dean has to be second only to Michael. They named the new UNC home gym (20,000 seats) after him. It's the Dean E. Smith Center, but everyone in Chapel Hill calls it the Dean Dome. Smith's daughter, Kristen, was a high school classmate of my niece, which is why Dean was at the wedding. I made sure to introduce Sam to the living legend, and we got Dean to tell stories about recruiting Jordan when his Airness was a high school student in Wilmington, North Carolina. "He was a late bloomer, but we thought he'd be able to play in the ACC," said Dean.

A few hours after we stopped listening to Dean, the late-night dancing was in full hip-hop swing. I noticed Sam making repeated trips to the bar with his cousins. Most of the cousins were over 21, but it was pretty clear that the bartenders didn't care. After one of Sam's visits, I asked the barkeep what the young man in front of me had ordered.

"Rum and Coke," said the polite man in the bow tie.

This was not much of a dilemma for me. I did the math and realized that Sam was already past the age when I'd first made a fool of myself drinking screwdrivers (vodka and Tang, sometimes) at Holy Cross. The legal drinking age was just about to switch to 18 when I was a freshman in college, and we learned the old-fashioned way. We drank too much, collapsed into bed, felt the room spinning, then spent a good part of the night calling Looie on the big white telephone. The good news was that we never got in cars on those nights. Our binges were confined to campus. In this spirit, I was okay watching my underage son having a few rum and Cokes with his cousins. They weren't going to be getting into cars and it wasn't going to impact Sam's coaches or teachers back home in Newton. It was a controlled environment. Better he learn here than on a Friday night back home when he'd be getting into a car after having a few at some other kid's house. I did, however, think it was a little bold when Sam came up to me and asked me for a few bucks to tip the bartender. I appreciated his taking care of the help, but did he have to be so blatant about drinking in front of his parents?

My dad's advice on drinking was short and old-school Irish. He told me to never drink alone and never drink in the morning.

Sam's track career was screeching to a halt as the snow piled up outside. He attended one meet and finished third in the 300 meters. He said that qualified him for a letter, but it was pretty clear that he wasn't bound for the Olympic trials. I was amazed that he was able to compete at all. Newton traditionally has the best track team in the state, and all Shaughnessys apparently lack the DNA needed to fix cars, speak foreign languages, and win footraces.

I was forced to run cross-country when I was a sophomore in high school. Since we had no football team, Coach Fahey made it a fall requirement for boys hoping to play varsity basketball. It was the best way to get us in shape, but I was tortured. Cursed with asthma, heavy legs, and the Shaughnessy gene pool, I was the worst runner on our team. Daily training runs of five miles were routine. This was the autumn of 1968; "Hey Jude" was atop the charts, and the droning Paul tune served nicely inside my head as I plopped one sneaker in front of the other up and down the hills on the second and third holes of the Groton Country Club. The actual competitions were even more pathetic. My goal was to keep jogging—never walk. Sometimes there would be a fat kid on the other team who'd end up walking part of the course. I think I beat about five kids all season. My most embarrassing moment came at the end of the meet in Littleton, when everybody was already on the bus waiting to ride home while I was still out on the course. Truly. They'd already calculated the scores, handed out the medals, put their sweats back on, and boarded the bus when somebody noticed I was still at large. The bus was pulled up alongside the finish line, engine running, when I came out of the last cornfield to complete my race. I crossed the line, ran up the steps of the bus, collapsed into a seat, and we were on our way back home.

Little has changed in adulthood. For the last twenty-four years, I have run one mile per day. Almost every day. I am the Cal Ripken Jr. of twelve-minute milers. Starting on New Year's Day in 1983, when I was in a hotel in downtown Los Angeles, I committed to running a mile a day. It was one of those rare resolutions that stuck. I remember seeing calendar pages from 1982 strewn around the streets of LA when I started the routine. It was my first year of married life, I was on the West Coast for the Rose Bowl and some Celtic games, and I was feeling a little fat. Almost every day since, I have run exactly one mile. Six minutes out. Six minutes back. I have run in Dealey Plaza in Dallas, in downtown Madrid, the streets of Sydney, the rocky coast of Ireland, Luxembourg Garden in Paris, and—most days—the Hunnewell Hill section of Newton. I ran the night Sam was born and the morning we found out about Kate's leukemia. When Kate was at Children's Hospital, I'd run down Brookline Ave., the only twelve minutes of the day I'd leave her side. There were days when I substituted basketball or swimming, but a short workout was mandatory, and I have missed only four times since '83, not once since '94. That's over 8,000 miles. A marathon a month. Across the country and back, just like Forrest Gump. And I have never had the urge to run faster or farther. Don't even ask.

My diaries disclosed more sad secrets of slowness. My high school mile time was eight minutes and twenty-five seconds. Sam runs one in 6:30. I was clocked at 7.1 seconds in the 50-yard dash. Sam ran 60 yards in 6.9 seconds at Stanford. Pretty amazing considering that I was six-one, 155 pounds and he's five-ten, 190.

Weight was something I was warning him about during these interminable months between baseball seasons. With no basketball and no track, I worried about Sam getting too big. A coach who recruits a Trot Nixon type doesn't want to see John Kruk showing up in September. With this in mind, I reminded Sam that he was about to officially become the fattest person in the family. After dropping some holiday weight, I burst into his bedroom before school one morning and dragged him to the scale. I was 193. He was 193.6.

Sam got a letter from the St. Louis Cardinals. "Congratulations on being identified as a future prospect by the St. Louis Cardinals!" wrote a New Jersey scout named Koby Perez. There was a lengthy questionnaire, and the scout's letter said Sam should fill it out and "consider this a job application for your dream career." Sam asked me what he should answer in the portion that inquired about his signability in the event he was drafted by the Cardinals. We both knew this wasn't going to be a problem, but it was fun talking about it anyway.

In lieu of basketball and track, he was going to the gym regularly and the baseball players were gathering informally for indoor captain's practices three times a week. Along with his pal Mike Huberman, he was also coaching a team of seventh-grade basketball players at the Boys Club. They called it "working with the little people."

At Sam's urging, I went to one of the games and watched the boys coach the little people. It was odd to see young parents talking to my son about their children. Sam and Mike had a young girl on their team. They also had a player named Elvis. "Pretty sure that's his real name," said Sam.

It pleased me that I didn't have to tell Sam to make sure the less-talented kids got a lot of playing time. A lifetime of playing ball teaches you the need for democracy at the lower levels. There'll be time for winning later on. You could tell that Sam and

Mike really enjoyed delivering instructions and making substitutions. They even had a sense of humor about it. When Elvis gave Mike some lip at halftime, Mike laughed, pointed to the door, and said, "Elvis, leave the building."

I have always found people who volunteer to coach kids to be among the best of our society. Sure, there's the occasional blowhard who's just there to advance the greatness of his own child, but for the most part these men and women are selfless and sincere. They donate time in an age when minutes and hours are precious and few. These coaches drive around with the bats, balls, and batting helmets rattling in their trunks. They leave work early and stay late to work with our kids. They make fifteen phone calls anytime it rains. They endure obnoxious players and parents. And they do it for the doughnut. It is an avocation that seems to attract a lot of cops and firefighters. Teachers, too, of course. These volunteer coaches can make a lasting impression on our sons and daughters. Forty years removed from the Groton town field, I still remember a lean man with a withered right arm who managed to hit one-armed fungoes while smoking a cigarette and expanding our vocabularies. All at the same time.

February

I T SEEMED TO ME that life was too easy for Sam. These were the final months of his high school career, and I worried he wasn't prepared for college and life thereafter. He seemed spoiled and apparently stress-free, and his routine was outrageously easy. He would get up at 7 A.M., less concerned about parking spots than he'd been in September, cruise to school, collect his B's without much effort, and sleep a good part of most afternoons. It had been seven months since he last played on a team. He managed to work out regularly at the local YMCA and ran regularly at the captain's practices. He coached the little people on Saturdays. But there was too much downtime, sitting at the computer on the second floor or slouching on the couch watching *Seinfeld* reruns and *SportsCenter*. And all the while, thin, smart girls with shiny hair continued to drift in and out of our home, watching TV and making brownies with him. Nice life. No worries about money, grades, zits, datelessness, athletic performance, or where he would be matriculating next year. No apparent edge or conflict. Could this be a good thing? Were we looking at a future business leader or had we created a lazy, selfish monster who would be incapable of sticking things out when life wasn't so easy someday?

I was ridiculously busy in my final months of high school in

1971. There was the stress of where I'd be going to college and how we were going to pay for it. I was writing a weekly sports column for the local newspaper, working twenty to twenty-five hours a week at the ice cream stand, playing varsity basketball and baseball, serving as class president, applying for scholarship aid, shoveling snow and mowing the lawn, and constantly worrying about getting rejected when I found the courage to ask someone to dance (as a result of this experience, Shaughnessy girls were mandated to say yes to any boy who asked at a high school dance. Give the guy a break and dance with him one time—unless he made the mistake of starting off with a slow dance).

Looking back at my diaries, I am stunned at the immaturity on those pages. At the same time, I'm amazed at the responsibility I was given. Norm Johnson, the owner and CEO of Johnson's Drive-In and a father of four children, trusted me to shut down and lock up his ice cream and hamburger establishment on slow weeknights in the fall and spring. This entailed snuffing out deep-fat fryers that could have exploded and burned the joint down if not done properly. It also meant locking all the doors and carrying the cash drawer up the hill to Mr. Johnson's porch, where I would place it in the dark breezeway. I was 16 years old, and this man put his entire life's work in my trembling hands on a regular basis. Would anybody dare do that today?

My chosen profession introduces me to a lot of successful people who worked hard (okay, probably not Manny Ramirez) to earn their place in the world, and it made me wonder about the SS *Cruise Ship* gliding through senior year with Sam on board.

Steve Burton is a talented, fortyish television sportscaster in Boston. He's one of five children of the late Ron Burton, a saint of a man who played professional football then dedicated his life to helping underprivileged young people from the city. Steve is handsome, athletic, and charming. As a high schooler, Steve was thrown out of St. Mark's, one of the more prestigious private schools in greater Boston. He got a letter from the headmaster informing him of his dismissal and had to take the embarrassing missive to his parents, who immediately directed him to the local public high school, Framingham North. There, Steve rallied and put together a resumé that led to his acceptance at Northwestern University. Today, he's a locally famous television personality with a wife and four children.

A few years ago, Steve was asked to a make an appearance at the school that bounced him all those years earlier, and he gladly returned to the scene of his humiliation. (It reminded me a little of when I was asked to return to Groton to speak to the National Honor Society—a club that rightfully denied me membership back in the day.) After speaking to the St. Mark's students, Burton was pulled aside by a schoolteacher who told him something he had never known.

"It turned out my dad had asked them to throw me out of the school," said Burton. "It was his wake-up call to me. He'd requested that they send me the letter, and he knew I'd have to take it to him. And he never told me. Not even twenty years later. It turned out that it was the best thing that ever happened to me. It forced me to get my act together. It was tough love."

Indeed. Could I do that? Probably not. I worry too much about my kids' happiness. As a result, they've rarely waited for things and suffered little. As far as a dad can tell, anyway. Like I said—too easy.

At Super Bowl XL in Detroit, I interviewed Isaiah Kacyvenski, a 28-year-old Seattle Seahawks linebacker. Nothing easy about this young man's life. He grew up in Endicott, New York, the youngest of five children. His mom was raised in an orphanage, and his dad was an alcoholic who beat the kids and failed to support the family. Kacyvenski remembered living in a tent in somebody else's backyard. He remembered combing through Dumpsters for food, and the embarrassment of watching his mom ridiculed for pushing food stamps across the counter at the local market. He got free lunches at school and that, too, was embarrassing. His dad would pummel him for no reason at all. When he was 9, Isaiah listened to the 1986 Super Bowl on the radio and made up his mind that he was going to be a football player. He set his sights on Notre Dame and became one of the best high school players in America. But Notre Dame never called. When he was a senior in high school, on the morning of a state tournament football game, he got the news that his mother was killed in a car crash. Kacyvenski was set to accept a scholarship to the University of Connecticut when Harvard coach Tim Murphy called. It seemed like a stretch, but Kacyvenski had a 98.6 grade point average, and Murphy convinced him that Harvard would change his life. And so he went. And he graduated cum laude. Meanwhile, his dad went on the wagon and Isaiah made him apologize for what he'd done to their family. Then he sent his father to Harvard to wear his cap and gown and accept his diploma while Isaiah went through the paces of mini-camp with the Seahawks. Six years later, Dave Kacyvenski sat in the stands at Ford Field and watched his Harvard grad son play in the Super Bowl.

Now *that* is a high school athlete who's got a story with some edge.

There is guilt in taking care of your kids too well. Making it too easy. My father endured long, uncomfortable commutes on streetcars from Cambridge to Boston College High School. He mastered Latin and somehow paid his way though Boston College with Depression dollars. He worked . . . and waited. No entitlements. No instant handouts from Mom and Dad. And let's not forget Marilou's dad, who was on a boat somewhere in the Panama Canal waiting to invade Japan when he was 19 years old in 1945.

When I got back from the Super Bowl in early February, I sat down with Sam and asked him what he was stressed about. He said he couldn't think of anything except baseball. We both knew there wasn't much pressure to perform in this final season, because his college situation was set. He wouldn't be worrying about impressing coaches and scouts every time he walked to the plate. By my math, that would make him stress-free for another twelve to fourteen months. And it bothered me. But I figured maybe it was my problem.

And then came an awakening. In February. During school vacation.

I was in Florida with the Red Sox—the twenty-seventh spring training of my writing career. Sam had made the trip with me in the previous three years. During one of the quiet Fort Myers mornings, before any players arrived, he'd gotten batting tips from Sox coach Ron Jackson—the same man who worked magic with David Ortiz and Manny Ramirez. "Papa Jack" became Sam's hitting guru, and any time Sam needed a pep talk I'd take him to Fenway to listen to the master. But there was no spring training in Florida for Sam in 2006. He was draft-eligible, committed to Boston College, and it would be risky for the Red Sox and for BC if word leaked that a high school senior was practicing at the big league facility. At this hour, we all knew Sam wasn't any kind of a professional prospect, but he'd risk losing his college eligibility if he spent any time in the Sox cages during senior year.

I'd been in Florida for a couple of days when Marilou called on a Tuesday morning to tell me things I never knew about my son. Sam had come home, drunk—in a taxi—at 3 A.M. The vodka he'd guzzled proved to be sodium pentothal, and from 3 A.M. to 5 A.M., Sam poured himself out as he sat in our cold, dark kitchen.

A line of new truths, one after another.

He'd been at a party and gotten into a fight with one of his best friends... They'd avoided another party at a "trouble" house where the cops regularly visited ... Just about all the kids had fake IDs and everybody could buy alcohol . . . He'd first smoked weed in the seventh grade . . . He always kept cab money in his pocket when he went to parties . . . He didn't know where his car keys were, but the car was still parked outside the home of the girl who had the party . . . He'd had his heart broken by his junior prom date, but they'd managed to become friends and she'd helped him through difficult times . . . Some of his friends thought he was bipolar and in need of medication . . . He'd suffered what he considered deep depression in the spring of his junior year when he slumped at the plate and worried he was overrated . . . He still had fits of crying . . . He wondered if drinking was hereditary—his roommate at Notre Dame told him he did not drink because his dad was an alcoholic . . . He worried about letting his teammates down when he underper-formed . . . He would always love Manny, the Legion coach who stuck by him when he was 15 years old, trying to keep up with college kids . . . He loved baseball bats as much as his mom loved books . . . Buddhist teachings were helping him cope.

Sam went to bed at 5 A.M. Marilou heard him throwing up a few hours later. She got him some aspirin and a cold washcloth, then let him sleep it off. Late in the afternoon, they went to get the car and he kept a sweatshirt hood over his head during the silent drive. He still didn't know where his keys were. Someone might have taken them from him as a safety measure. He was al-lowed to go to the North-South basketball game that night. He was hoping somebody would return his keys.

I spent the day in Florida writing about Manny Ramirez and wondering how I could be so clueless about my own son. I was the champion of telling everyone that we never really know what our teenagers are doing, and yet I'd been blind-sided by Sam's admissions. Teenagers smoking pot and getting drunk hardly qualifies as breaking news, but I'd duped myself into thinking that Sam steered clear of it all because he was so committed to baseball. Turns out nobody steers clear of it all, not at a suburban high school of 2,200 students. Not now. Not in 1971 either, come to think of it.

All this stuff went on when I was in high school, but I pretty much missed the whole thing. The permissive era of Sex, Drugs, and Rock 'n' Roll went on without me. No beers. Not one. A little vodka with Heather Stoddart, but not enough to put my head into a toilet bowl. No drugs. Not even a joint. Fear of parents and police, I guess. I was so clean, the bad guys used to ask me to ride shotgun just in case they got pulled over by the cops. Like some force field of innocence, my mere presence in an automobile would make the rest of the kids in the car above suspicion. It was the same at school. I could walk the corridors without a hallway pass and never be challenged. When I dropped out of an advanced math class, the principal called me into the office to find out what was wrong with the *teacher*.

Unfortunately, the young women of my day had the same sense of my Opie wholesomeness. Too safe. High school girls love bad boys, which meant that none of them loved me. The *moms* loved me, and we all know what an aphrodisiac that is for a 16-year-old girl. I was a complete nonthreat. Kathy Sullivan's mom sent us off on our date telling me it didn't matter what time I got Kathy home because I'd been such a cute baby. If I'd been dating the moms of Groton in 1971, I could have been Warren Beatty, but this got me nowhere with the cheerleaders and field hockey players of my dreams.

When I was a senior in high school, arriving home drunk and carless at 3 A.M. would have triggered the end of life as I knew it. (Let's not even talk about the taxicab—to my knowledge there has never been a taxi on the streets of Groton.) Grounded? Try house arrest. Hard labor. Shame, shame, and more shame. Now here we were, thirty-five years later, handing Sam some Tylenol, letting him out again the next night, and patting him on the back because he'd taken a taxi instead of driving. It was a decidedly new-school response. Sure, we were planning on meting out some punishment, but the first reaction was relief. He wasn't in a serious car accident. He wasn't arrested. He hadn't been kicked off the baseball team. He hadn't lost his partial scholarship. Baby boomer parents of this century tend to go light on the tough love. We are reminded that we might lose our connection with our kids altogether if we come down too hard. And so we cave in.

Suddenly, we had a new goal for our last child: see him through senior year without any catastrophe. Get across the finish line without scandal or disgrace.

Do the math. Three kids. Thirteen years of public schools per child. This was our thirty-ninth and final year in the Newton school system. There were four months to go.

I didn't talk to Sam the day after his barf bag bacchanal. I figured I'd wait until I got back from Florida. It was a little awkward because I'd scored some serious lumber for him at the Red Sox camp. Friends in the Sox clubhouse set aside some of the bats left behind by players who'd been traded, released, or had left via free agency. I had maple models once used by Doug Mirabelli, Edgar Renteria, Bill Mueller, Kevin Millar, and John Olerud.

The Bay State League, one of the better baseball conferences in Massachusetts, uses wood bats because Wellesley lefty Billy Hughto was almost killed by a line drive hit off an aluminum bat in the 1990s. Hughto was on the mound when a shot back to the hill smashed his skull and bounded to the outfield. He was helicoptered to a hospital in Boston, where doctors successfully relieved the pressure on his brain and saved his life. A couple of years later, the Bay State League switched to wood and hitters soon learned they had to do things the hard way. Old school.

It seemed indulgent and inappropriate to come home with big league wood bats in the wake of Sam's vacation behavior, but

I was feeling a little guilty myself. It was unfair for me to have assumed that he was stress-free.

Now all this. Drugs. Alcohol. Bad judgments. Sam was going to be told that some friends and their homes would be off-limits. And the drinking simply had to stop. A year earlier, Newton's best hitter forfeited his senior season because of two alcohol violations.

Eligibility and scandal aside, I was disappointed that we hadn't been able to talk about the drinking thing. And like a lot of parents, I knew I'd been a poor role model. He'd seen too much drinking in our home. Too many parties with adults getting too woozy. How could kids not notice? Now my son was asking if alcoholism could be inherited. Not good.

It was also shocking to hear that Sam had girl trouble. Again, I'd missed the signs of stress and assumed that relationships were easy for him. I'd joked about his being an International Man of Mystery. I'd read my pathetic diary entries and discovered a lonely loser, unlucky at love. Turned out Sam had heartbreak of his own. Turned out 18 is 18. Some things are universal, no matter what it looks like from the sidelines.

I flew home from Florida on a Friday night for the final weekend of February, the final weekend of Sam's vacation. He was awake when I came in the front door after midnight, and he didn't groan when I told him to take my heavy bag to my second-floor office. I'd managed to fit eight bats into the suitcase, wrapping them in a towel in an effort to prevent pine tar from staining my clothes. We still weren't talking about his risky business from earlier in the week, but I had made it a condition that he clean his room before he got a look at the bats. Leverage can be a wonderful thing. By Sam's standards, his room looked okay when I inspected it, and so he was allowed to harvest the Wonderboy wood in my American Tourister. Looking like the wine connoisseur Paul Giamatti played in *Sideways,* he removed the bats one by one, holding each one aloft to inspect the model numbers and wood grain. The Renteria bat was last, and we both laughed when it came out of the bag with a pair of my white briefs clinging to the sticky handle like a shredded sail on a broken mast. "This would be a tough one to explain," Sam said as he held the bat by the barrel and unsuccessfully attempted to shake off the stubborn underwear.

Nothing was said about the party scare. Not yet. And everything was put on hold again the next day when we got a phone call from Sarah telling us that she'd been hit in the face with a softball bat during an intra-squad scrimmage at Harvard. She'd caught a foul pop while catching and was struck in the eye socket by the on-deck hitter when she went to retrieve her mask after the play. Six hours later, seven of us took stitched-up Sarah to our neighborhood steak restaurant, the Stockyard. The poor kid was devastated. She's been told there was a crack in her orbital bone, and it looked as if she was going on the disabled list just as her season was about to begin. Sarah was third-string catcher and had only a couple of at-bats in her first two years with the Crimson, but she'd been working hard and hoped to get more playing time in 2006. Now it looked like her junior season was going to be a wash. It reminded us all of the fragile nature of this sports business. You're always just one unlucky break away from a season on the shelf, something I know would have made Sam deeply depressed and probably would have put me into therapy, too.

We all agreed that the most amazing component of Sarah's injury was that she'd been struck by someone swinging a bat . . . *and it was not her brother!* On the day Sarah was injured, I counted twenty-eight of Sam's bats in Kate's room.

Two days after I got home, the day after Sarah's injury, Marilou and I took Sam to lunch on Charles Street in downtown Boston. Again, decidedly new school. Not only was Sam not getting punished, but we were also buying him lunch, for God's sake. *Congratulating* him on having the wisdom not to drink and drive; we were practically giving him a parade. As long as we were kissing ass, why not just give him a couple cases of beer and a hundred bucks for his next five cab rides? Yeesh.

Ever modern and sensitive, we resisted the urge to blast his behavior. Instead, we told him we'd made mistakes. We reminded him of how close he'd come to blowing everything—losing his place at Boston College and possibly losing his high school baseball season. He admitted, "I went a little overboard," but there wasn't much contrition. Teens in 2006 are not easily embarrassed. These are teenagers who don't bother to put feet back on the floor and straighten out their clothes if you walk in on them when they are draped all over one another while watching TV.

We were all stuck with the ever-popular notion that everybody was doing it and let's just try to get to graduation without a tragic episode. Sam said in some ways it was better that he and his friends were learning about drugs and alcohol now, because they'd be less likely to go wild when presented with the ultimate freedoms that greet every freshman in every dorm in America each September. I was less than satisfied with the session but kept telling myself that there wasn't much parenting left to do. At this point, the kids are pretty much formed. They're soon to be on their own. They're going to have to live with the choices they make.

I was reminded of Chazz Palminteri's brilliant *A Bronx Tale,* in which the teenage Calogero Anello says, "Remember, the saddest thing in life is wasted talent and the choices that you make will shape your life forever." I'd made Sam watch the 1993 coming-of-age flick when we were together in Florida during his junior year, and he'd made it must viewing for some of his friends. Now those celluloid lessons were hitting him headfirst, like the barrel of a metal bat into the orbital socket.

Meanwhile, as we lurched toward March, the Newton North boys' basketball team—the one Sam wasn't on—continued to steamroll every team in eastern Massachusetts. They won their last home game to improve to 18-0 in early February. The final home game features a nice tradition: each senior is introduced by the head coach, then crosses the court to embrace his parents and present his mom with flowers. The 2005–2006 team had seven of Sam's classmates. Alexis's mom and dad were both on hand for the occasion. I hadn't seen them in the same place together since a Saturday morning soccer game when the boys were about 8 years old.

We had some good news on Alexis: he was accepted by Emmanuel College during the February break. He also made his first career start—no small event for a kid who'd been buried on the bench behind Corey and Anthony.

I first saw Corey Lowe when Sam was playing on a fourth-grade travel team. In those days, Corey was the best player on the team, the best player on the court in just about every game. A couple of years later, Sam was teammates with Anthony Gurley, who was equally spectacular. It fascinates me to see these young men, six years later, dominating our entire region. I've been going to basketball games for over forty-five years and like to think I know something about talent. So why was I so dismissive of these kids when they were little? Sure, they were good, I reasoned, but every team has one kid who is better than the others. Kids like that are all over the place and as the years unfold, those kids find out there are better players in other towns. They fall back to the pack. Not this time. Anthony and Corey were just as overpowering in high school as they were on those sixth-grade travel teams. I wondered if they'd be able to keep it up when they moved to the next level. I spoke with Chris Paul when the New Orleans Hornets came to the Garden and the soon-to-be-named NBA Rookie of the Year assured me that young Anthony was ready to play for the Deacons. "Tell him we need him right away," said the NBA star. Heady stuff for a high school kid.

Corey had grown up in Newton, while Anthony came to us via the Metco program from the heart of Boston, Roxbury. Unlike Corey, Anthony had crashed regularly in our home. Another brother for Sarah, Kate, and Sam. He wasn't a weekly presence like Alexis, but in the years before they all got their driver's licenses, Anthony slept in every bed on the second floor. Sam and the girls called him "Ant." He'd announce himself in the kitchen with "That sure smells good, Marilou." We've watched him grow up. Literally. Last time he was in the kitchen, I made him take off his shoes and look me in the eye, and I conceded that he is finally taller than me. A legitimate six foot three and still growing, Anthony is an explosive scorer who can create his shot off the dribble as well as any high schooler I've seen. Prep scouting publications ranked him the twenty-sixth-best recruit in the country in 2006. His mom drives for the MBTA and his dad runs a car detail shop in Boston. Big Tony Gurley tells me he'll be seeing a lot of games at Wake in the next few years—he's planning to rent an apartment in Winston-Salem. The *Globe* ran a lengthy profile of Anthony just before the state tournament, and it was predictably gushing. The feature included a photo of Anthony getting on a bus before 7 A.M. By any measure, Anthony was one of the best high school players in the history of our state.

In my world, you see thousands of kids playing ball through the years and many of them think they'll be in the NBA someday. It is the Great Myth. According to the National Alliance of Youth Sports, only one out of every 30,000 high school basketball players ever makes it to the NBA. But I was beginning to wonder if maybe Anthony was going to be that one in 30,000. In any case, I looked forward to watching him on television in the next few years. I knew I'd see him at the foul line in his Wake jersey and think of him making pancakes in our kitchen.

"I wish he was going to BC," said Sam. "We could have been roommates and that would have been so much fun."

Winning close games against good teams, the Tigers were 22-0 at the end of February and ranked first in eastern Massachusetts. This was about the same time I got a canceled check that I'd written out to the Newton North athletic department. It was check for $125 dated November 28—Sam's basketball user fee. I knew this was a mistake. Sam had only been at tryouts for two days. I called Athletic Director T. J. Williams, and he said we could apply the fee toward Sam's baseball season. He explained that there was no user fee if a player quit during tryouts or was cut from the team. I told T. J. that Sam neither quit nor was cut. He was "run off," encouraged not to try out for the team. Big difference, and I was still bitter, still stinging a little, as the North team stormed toward another state championship and another appearance at the Boston Garden. Sam, of course, had long since made his peace with that situation and was happy to sit in the stands and yell his head off with his classmates.

Anthony, Alexis, Sam, and Nick Wolfe, one of the starting pitchers on the baseball team, were all at the house when I came home on the last night of February. I congratulated Anthony on the *Globe* article and Lex on his admission to Emmanuel. Sam placed a whopping order with Wings Express, and we all sat around the TV room eating steak tips and chicken wings before making the short drive to Boston College, where the Wake Forest Deacons were playing the Boston College Eagles. It reminded me of the old days when we'd pile a bunch of sixth graders into our old Volvo wagon for a trip to a travel team basketball game. In 2006, I was carrying more than a thousand pounds of humanity in my Camry and Anthony was too tall for the back seat.

Universal tip to all parents: if you want to learn what's going on with your kids, put your child in a car loaded with his peers, then shut up and drive. You will hear more truths than you'll get in a month of those dinner conversations where you ask, "How'd things go at school today?" In the car, toting kids to games, you might as well be Patrick Swayze in *Ghost*. You are invisible. Fortunately, this doesn't change even when they are seniors in high school.

On the drive over to BC, Nick said, "Sam, tomorrow's the first day of March. What do you say? Breakfast, lunch, and dinner?"

"I couldn't do that," said Sam. "Maybe lunchtime."

Turns out they had given up fast food for the month of February. Nice idea. Four weeks had passed and of course I never noticed.

I bumped into NBC's Tim Russert at the BC-Wake game. His son, Luke, was a student at Boston College, and I knew Tim had found it difficult to watch his only son go off to college after eighteen years at home.

"It was the most difficult six weeks of my life," said Russert. "For eighteen years I'm screaming about wet towels on the bathroom floor. All of a sudden, there are no more wet towels and you want wet towels on the floor."

March

THE RED SOX PLAYED their annual spring training game against Boston College in the first week of March. Ace pitcher Curt Schilling, the big blowhard himself, got the nod for the start against the college kids and mowed them down, allowing no runs on one hit in four breezy innings. BC's first baseman, Dave Preziosi, a fifth-year senior, got Schill's attention right out of the gate when he took a Reggie Jacksonesque cut at a first-pitch fastball and fouled it back to the screen. The kid later admitted that he was going for a home run and had no problem when Schill buzzed him, up and in, on the next pitch. It occurred to me that with a little luck, Sam could be in that situation in another year. I doubt big Curt would show any mercy pitching to freshman Sam Shaughnessy.

Schilling hit a young player in the head the first time he faced major league batters a week later. The twenty-five-year-old Pirates outfielder Chris Duffy sustained a minor concussion when Schilling's 90-mile-per-hour fastball knocked the helmet off his head on an 0-2 pitch. After the game, Schilling said, "That ball should not have hit him. You've got to be able to get out of the way of that . . . there's just no way that they shouldn't be able to get out of the way of that pitch. If they're not comfortable in the box, the body will get out of the way."

It was appalling—somewhat like friends of Dick Cheney blaming Cheney's hunting pal for not getting his face out of the way of the vice president's shotgun blast. The Pirates were not pleased when informed of Schilling's remarks.

Same here. As a parent of a ballplayer who soon was going to be playing at a fairly high level, I was beginning to view things a little differently. I was suddenly sympathetic to young players struggling just to get one day in the big leagues. Someday my own son might be one of the faceless minions we ignore at the minor league complex every year at spring training.

Seeing a batter take one off the helmet had new meaning, too. Sam had been hit quite a few times in his career but never on the head. It's not something you talk about. I presume trapeze performers don't have many discussions about falling off the high wire. Cops don't talk about the prospect of getting shot on the job. It's something that's always there, but it's bad luck to talk about it in advance. I knew Sam would have his moment of truth and there was no way to know how he'd react. A good hitter who digs in at home plate is going to be drilled sooner or later. Pitchers need to take back the inside of the plate and fear is part of their arsenal. That's what Schilling was talking about.

While I was in Florida watching the Red Sox, the Newton North basketball team kept winning. I checked in with Sam on a regular basis and was happy to hear that Alexis was getting more playing time and even drilled a couple of three-pointers in a state tourney semifinal. Anthony and Corey were still dominating, but Sam's Metco brother was making some big shots under a lot of pressure—and a lot of college coaches were watching. It was Alexis's dream to play basketball in college and I was beginning to think he might be able to pull it off.

Newton North's class of '06 returned to the Boston Garden. Playing in front of 10,000 fans, they topped Lawrence Central, and the seniors had some great things to say after the victory.

"This is our senior year, so we're all thinking when we come out here that this could be our last game," said Corey after raining twenty-five points through the Garden nets. "Everybody's going to go out there and play as hard as we can, and so far we've won every game, so it's working."

Jason Riffe, another senior shooter and one of the football studs, said, "It's still nice to come to the Garden because you don't get too many chances to come here. A lot of kids don't get to come here once and now it's twice for us. We still wanted to soak it up."

Soak it up. Here was a kid after my own heart.

In 1969, in anticipation of Groton High's best basketball team in years, I wrote a diary/book on our season and called it *Throw Up for Glory*. I can't really take credit for that title because I stole it from Bill Russell's seminal sports tome, *Go Up for Glory*. I'd checked Russell's book out of the high school library when I was a sophomore (in 2004, I found that same book on the shelf of the new Groton-Dunstable Regional High School library and my sign-out card was still tucked into the sleeve inside the back cover) and figured Big Bill wouldn't mind if I appropriated his title. A modern examination of my never-published work reveals this passage written in the winter of 1969–70: "It's all starting to kind of scare me — 10-1, seven in a row, league leaders, Boston newspapers, and the aura of the Boston Garden. We could really go there."

We did not make it to the Boston Garden. Clinton High beat us in the central Mass. quarterfinals. That didn't stop me from sending *Sports Illustrated* a sample chapter of *Throw Up for Glory*, generously offering them first-serial rights. A few weeks later, I got a letter (which I still have, of course) from an associate editor politely informing me that the magazine was not in the business of publishing the diaries of high school basketball players. Their loss. *Throw Up for Glory* could have been *A Sea-*

son on the Brink or a *Friday Night Lights*. The movie soundtrack would have featured Norman Greenbaum's "Spirit in the Sky."

I did not write a book about our senior hoop season at Groton, but I did cover our high school teams in a weekly column for local newspaper the *Public Spirit*. Covering five or six towns, the *Spirit* is one of those classic rags featuring lots of photos of guys shaking hands at the Rotary Club, alongside birth and wedding announcements, and news of when it will be okay to burn leaves on the curb in front of your house. In the 1970s, the best part of the *Public Spirit* was the weekly "police news" featuring reports of cats in trees and "suspicious" vehicles parked on quiet streets. It was fun to see who got busted for drunk driving, and in the 1970s, there seemed to be a lot of reports of young people caught with "a controlled substance, to wit: marijuana."

I was paid fifteen cents per inch for my sports reports. This meant an extra twenty to thirty bucks a month, plus I could get my friends' names in the paper. I could exaggerate the victories and make the losses go away. Since I was playing in many of the games, I used a pseudonym, "Lancer," which I selected because that was John F. Kennedy's code name with the secret service. Doubt many other 17-year-old kids knew that in 1970.

Intrepid "Lancer" found himself in a bind early in our basketball season, when I choked on a couple of free throws and almost cost us a game. We were playing on a Friday night in Littleton and, per usual, I was on the bench for just about the entire game. With about a minute left, our best player was injured as he was fouled. We didn't have any timeouts left, which meant that a benchwarmer would have to take the free throws after the brief delay. Coach Fahey sent me to the line. I could make twenty-four out of twenty-five free throws in practice. But this was different. I was cold and nervous. And I cared too much. I was not clutch. We were down by a point and I was going to the line for two and the gym was packed. My first attempt rimmed out. It was a good miss, but still a miss. Naturally, I choked on the second one, heaving a brick that barely drew iron. That was it for me. Back to the bench. When play resumed, our star was back on the floor and another teammate, Dave Bond, saved my ass with a put-back at the buzzer. Lancer's subsequent game story featured all the bloody details, including Dan Shaughnessy choking on a couple of free throws, but Coach Fahey got hold of the unedited copy and had my embarrassing performance expunged.

Seeing Newton North at the Boston Garden three and a half decades later reminded me just how special such an experience would have been in my *Public Spirit* world. This time around, of course, I could have been the doofus dad with the mini-cam, capturing the moment of Sam doing lay-up drills on the Garden floor, vicariously experiencing what I'd missed in 1970. Instead, it was our fourth kid—Alexis—who got into the game and drained another three pointer. Anthony scored twenty-four. I remembered the days when these kids were playing pickup in our driveway. I could post-up little Anthony when he was 10. Not now.

Reinforced by books and cinema, the image of fathers and sons "having a catch" stands as the traditional American parent-child sports connection. In my world, it's one-on-one basketball. My one-on-one basketball games against Sam have been the best barometer of my ever-fading place in the competitive sports. It's probably the same when you teach your son to play golf or tennis. In the early years, you do as you please and emphasize instruction. You win anytime you want and occasionally let the little guy get close to boost his spirit. Then your child grows, becomes more competent and competitive, and the games are suddenly contested. You still prevail, but every year you're getting older and slower and your son is getting bigger and better. Finally, sadly, like lines intersecting on a graph, your son beats you at your own game and you know it's only going to get worse. It's ascent versus descent and the trend is irreversible. Sam beat me in the driveway for the first time when he was about 15. I know now I'll never beat him again. Anthony probably shot past me by the time he was 12.

On the night that North won at the Garden, all but twelve points were scored by members of the class of 2006. There was no way our coach was going to replace this senior class. Seven seniors played on North's history-making squad and four of them had been part of the football team that made it to the Eastern Massachusetts Super Bowl. These characters were creating quite a legacy for themselves. We could only hope their heads wouldn't get too big and they wouldn't do anything stupid before graduation.

I took Sam out to dinner at the Stockyard the night after the Garden game and used the opportunity to cover a number of subjects. I asked him about the two warnings he'd gotten from school (extending his four-year streak). The missive from his creative writing teacher read, "Quality of work is inconsistent, more effort needed, needs to bring materials to class." (Kate wondered, "Materials? For writing class? Would that be a pen?") Sam said there was no problem. He said there would be no C's on his transcript come graduation. Satisfied with that, I asked about a story in the paper that recounted the arrests of two of his classmates, twin brothers, who'd been caught making fake IDs (reminding me of the famed Savage brothers in *Mystic River*). Sam said the going rate for the phony driver's licenses was $120, but he'd rejected the opportunity to purchase one. I told him it seemed like a lot of dough, but he explained that the twins incurred considerable start-up costs, including a high-quality printer, a laminator, and special paper. The boys were arrested while dumping their equipment. A local police officer told the newspaper, "It's the same penalty if you make fake IDs or you own one. It's a five-year felony . . . as prom and graduation season approaches,

Newton and surrounding towns don't need kids to be involved in this."

After a long pause, I asked Sam if—now that he'd seen his friends win at the Boston Garden again—he had any regrets about not being part of the basketball magic. He was shaking his head no before I finished the question.

After that, he took the opportunity to ask me how the book was coming. Sam knew about this project—I'd shown him the introduction before school started in September. We had a deal that he would not get to look at any of the material while the book was being written. I didn't want the book to influence his behavior in any way, and it appeared I'd succeeded in that department. But I knew he was probably worrying about disclosure of the night he "went a little overboard" during February vacation.

Changing the subject, I mentioned some unsettling neighborhood news. Mack, the beloved Australian shepherd owned by the Inskeep family across the street from our house, had been put down in the middle of March. No small episode in our cloistered corner of town, people brought food to the Inskeep home during their time of grief.

I've never been a guy for pets. My parents wouldn't let us have a dog or a cat, and I knew it was a waste of time to ask. Not surprisingly, as an adult I have the same attitude. It's simple: a person who grows up without pets doesn't want pets. And so it was easy to dismiss the request when our children were young. "Why do you need a dog?" I'd ask my little daughters. "You've got a little brother. Play with him. Sam will fetch."

My Fido frost melted quickly when Kate was diagnosed with leukemia. Who could say no to a brave little girl who wore a chemo backpack to school during her days of twenty-four-hour infusions? Kate didn't complain about ridiculously painful bone marrow tests or spinal taps. She played softball despite her skeletal frame. She turned baldness into an asset when she went out on Halloween as Charlie Brown. She bit her lip and stayed strong when we went to the funerals of little friends who didn't survive.

And I was going to say no when she asked for a dog?

Luke, a golden retriever puppy delivered from central casting, came into our home in 1994 when Kate was in the throes of treatment. I assumed Kate named him "Luke" because of leukemia, but it turned out she just liked the name. Sam was only 7 when we got the dog. He got a kick out of throwing tennis balls down our dead-end street and watching Luke do what came naturally: run like hell, scoop the ball with his mouth, then return with the slimed, fuzzy Wilson wedged between his teeth.

In Shaughnessy family folklore, it is an article of faith that Dad Dan will be on a work-related road trip whenever something bad happens. Cars break down, basements flood, toilets explode, kids get the mumps, teen son gets drunk and takes a cab home . . . Dad invariably is in some Marriott in Houston, Chicago, or New York. So naturally I was in New York City in September 2001 when Luke died.

It was an unspeakable ending. Due probably to lack of exercise (lack of retrieving, would that be ironic?), Luke got too heavy and morphed into a mule by the time he turned 7, when Sam was 13. On an otherwise routine Saturday afternoon, Luke had trouble breathing and needed medical attention. Marilou hoisted him into the rear compartment of our eggplant-colored Dodge minivan and drove to the veterinarian's office. Sam rode in the back with Luke. When she arrived at the vet's, she was told that they were not seeing emergency patients on the weekend and was referred to another animal hospital. She explained that our dog was in distress, but the young vet shrugged and said, "Sorry, that's our policy."

Marilou got back in the car and drove frantically toward Angell Memorial Hospital. Cradling Luke's head in the back of the van, Sam couldn't tell if his dog was breathing. He asked his mom to turn off the air conditioner so he could hear better. By then, Luke had stopped breathing. He died in Sam's arms.

I'd often wondered what that was like for Sam. He eventually told us in the form of an assignment for his creative writing teacher ("quality of work is inconsistent"). Sam wrote a story that concluded with a passage describing a young man holding his fiancée after she'd been mortally wounded by a random shot while riding the New York subway. "Steve laid with Jessica as she slowly died," Sam wrote. "As Steve could feel her breathing start to slow up, he . . . told her he would always love her. Moments later, Jessica died."

One thing high school authors are not . . . is subtle. If you don't believe me, I still have a longhand copy of *Throw Up for Glory*.

The Newton North boys' basketball team won its second straight state championship on Saturday, March 18, beating Holy Name of Worcester 67–58. Anthony scored twenty-seven points in his final high school game, and North finished 27-0, with thirty-two consecutive wins and a two-year record of 53-1. North became the first Division One state champ to run the table in seventeen years. Sam and his friends made the drive to Worcester for the final, which was somewhat anticlimactic after the Eastern Mass. final at the Garden.

The game in Worcester was a true community event. Captains from the class of 2005 came back and participated in a pregame ceremony to accept a state sportsmanship award at center court. Little kids asked the ballplayers for autographs. Most of the fans in the stands had watched these boys grow up and pass through the school system. Many were carpoolers and coaches at one time or another. When it was over, outgoing principal Jennifer Huntington hung medals around the neck of each player.

"I'll never forget this, not twenty years from now," Anthony told the *Globe*.

But there was some bad news in our house because Alexis

didn't get off the bench for more than a minute of that final game, and his mom said she couldn't get him out of bed the next morning. He'd been humiliated in front of his family and friends.

Two days after basketball season ended, indoor baseball try-outs were held on the first day of spring, a day when the greater Boston temperatures topped out at 38 degrees. Sam and fellow captains, J. T. Ross and James Greeley, had been holding informal, indoor practices for baseball players for more than a month, and they had a pretty good idea how the team was going to look. North had gone 12-8 in each of the prior two seasons, winning one game in the state tourney before shutting down for the summer. There was every reason to believe they'd make the tournament again, although they were unlikely to match the levels of success attained by the football and basketball teams.

Newton's head coach, Joe Siciliano, was observing his twentieth season as varsity baseball coach. An engaging math teacher and one-time ballplayer, nobody loved baseball more than the bespectacled Sis. He'd raised a gang of kids with his wife, Sandy, and their youngest son, Mark, was Sam's Legion teammate before going off to play college ball at Babson. Sis also served as longtime coach of the junior varsity basketball team, which meant Sam Shaughnessy was getting ready to play his sixth season under the man. Had to be a record. Thank God we all liked him.

I had a soft spot for Sis. It helped that we'd spent time together in the bleachers as parents when Mark Siciliano and Sam were Legion teammates. At those games, I'd learned how much the man loved baseball and how much he knew about the game. Sis was one of those guys you'd see raking the infield dirt at ten in the morning on a game day. And if it rained, he'd stand in the middle of the diamond like Charlie Brown, ignoring the deluge around him and saying, "Let's play two!" This was a 60-year-old man who wore a full uniform and *batting gloves* on game days. Like all the good high school coaches, he was also a keen student of the teenage mind. He knew how to discipline and he knew how to reward. You want to send a message to a good ballplayer? Take away his playing time. Bench him. That kid will remember not to swear or throw his helmet next time. Sam Shaughnessy was that kid more than once, and Sis put the hammer down by putting Sam's ass on the bench for the rest of the day. But our baseball coach could also be a softie. When his seniors played the last game of their baseball careers (for many if would be their last organized game ever), he made sure they all got in the game. Alexis Mongo would not have been paralyzed in bed, ashamed to come out of his room, the day after winning a state championship if he'd been a senior ballplayer playing for Joe Siciliano.

I made it home for a couple of days in late March, after the basketball team had won. It was a tense time at North. College envelopes were in the mail and kids were comparing stories. On a Friday night, Sam and I watched Boston College's basketball team lose to Villanova in the Sweet Sixteen. A ridiculous loss. We both knew BC should have won. Better than an intense parent-child conference, or a not-so-subtle dinner summit at the Golden Star, we covered a lot of stuff during the two-hour broadcast. During one of the timeouts, Sam asked me if there had been any envelope from Boston College in the daily mail. No.

I remembered three years earlier when Sarah was waiting for letters from Brown and Harvard, and how much that had dominated my thoughts and dreams. This was nothing like that. Sam was going to Boston College. It was a bag job. He'd signed the letter of intent. Marilou had wanted him to apply to the University of Connecticut as a backup, but Michael LaVigne reminded us that the letter of intent was a legally binding agreement and told her to save the $70 and take us all out for dinner. Good advice.

The next day, a few minutes after Sam left the house for a Saturday morning scrimmage, a packet from Boston College was pushed through the front door slot and landed with a thud on the floor of the breezeway. I'd planned to watch the scrimmage, and when I pulled into third lot just before noon, I had the BC package riding shotgun. I made my way to the aluminum bleachers adjacent to the visiting bench on the third base side.

Sitting in my usual spot, I noticed Dan Duquette walking behind the visitors' bench. Duquette had been general manager of the Red Sox during the 1990s and early 2000s. One of the architects of the Sox 2004 Championship team, he was the man who brought Pedro Martinez, Manny Ramirez, Jason Varitek, and Derek Lowe to the Red Sox. Duquette and I had been adversaries. I'd praised him occasionally but hammered him regularly, and now he was out of major league baseball, replaced by Theo Epstein.

Seeing Dan at the North ball field was weird. Our work had put us in high-profile conflict for almost a decade, but on this chilly Saturday we were just a couple of middle-aged dads, watching our sons play a meaningless scrimmage. Late in the game, Daniel Duquette was on the mound when Sam Shaughnessy came to bat. Young Duquette had retired all seven Newton batters he'd faced. Standing next to the former Sox GM, as the count ran to 1-1, I could no longer ignore the obvious and said, "Okay, Dan, here's the Duquette-Shaughnessy matchup. Gotta be stakes. What you do say—a lobster roll at the Stockyard?"

"Let's make it lunch at the Stockyard," said Duquette.

Just as those words left his mouth, young Daniel hung a curveball and Sam smacked a single into right-center field.

There was a pretty young girl in the stands, Emily. She'd been Sam's junior prom date, the second baseman/knockout who got all the attention whenever anybody looked at Sam's prom pictures. In the photo, Sam was wearing a newly minted Joseph Abboud suit, but photo viewers could not get past the stunning young girl in the black sequined prom dress. Emily and I chatted in the cold bleachers. She said BC was one of her top choices. She asked if Sam had heard anything and, slightly guiltily, I held up the envelope.

This was a classic example of over-parenting in this century. It was not my place to spread Sam's good news, and he should have been the one—not his dad—to deal with the delicate situation of telling Emily that he'd been accepted while she was still waiting. I still feel bad about it. (Emily wound up going to Wisconsin, a hot school for kids from Newton in 2006.)

Sam was lifted from the lineup in the late innings and I approached him while he worked alone in the batting cage down the right field line. Had this been a real game, such intervention would have been a clear-cut violation of parent-child game comportment. You never interact with your kid in the middle of a game. Never. Not even if the child is lying on the turf, holding a broken leg or a severed Achilles tendon. It just looks bad. It embarrasses your son or daughter and it's disrespectful to the coach. But this was a scrimmage and nobody was paying much attention and I had Sam's future under my armpit. Plus, it seemed fitting for Sam to tear open this envelope while his cleated feet were standing on the lawn where he'd earned his admission to this college.

He smiled and sighed when I gave him the envelope. Then he walked back toward the bench. He wanted to be with his teammates when he tore it open. A couple of minutes later, he sauntered back my way, gave me a thumbs-up signal, then stuffed the ripped envelope and its contents into my hand. He went back to the bench. I walked to my car and took a peek:

"Dear Mr. Shaughnessy: I am delighted to offer you admission to the Carroll School of Management at Boston College. From over 26,500 applicants you have been chosen to join the

2,250 students entering the class of 2010." At the bottom of the letter, next to the signature of Danielle S. Wells, assistant director of BC admissions, she'd written, "Congratulations, Sam . . . looking forward to seeing you out on the diamond."

Alexis got dropped off at North later that day and I drove him to our house. We talked about coach dissing him in the state final in Worcester. He said he'd been unable to enjoy the state championship celebration. We talked about college. He was still waiting to hear from his first choice, the University of Massachusetts at Amherst. Finances were going to be a problem, and he was probably going to have to take out some loans. I could see that the process was wearing him out.

I flew to California the next day, my last big trip before the start of Sam's baseball season. I'd told my boss that I wanted to take a lot of vacation time in April, May, and June. This was the last high school go-around for our last ballplayer and I didn't want to miss a moment. In California, I was housed at the Doubletree Suites in Santa Monica and my room looked out on the Santa Monica High School baseball field. I was in foul territory, about four hundred feet from home plate outside the right field line. A virtual high school baseball luxury box. Rick Monday, the first player selected in the first baseball draft of 1965, had been a lefty slugger at Santa Monica, and he could easily have put a ball through my window at the Doubletree. Looking out that window, day after day, I saw tall, rangy Californians sweating on the diamond and I thought about our boys back in Newton, wearing hooded sweatshirts in 40-degree temperatures.

The Samohi (Santa Monica High) Vikings played a home game against Hawthorne on the afternoon of my last full day in California. Wearing sunglasses, a gray T-shirt, and a black sports jacket, I strolled over to the field and set up behind the backstop. It was nice to be able to watch from so close, a luxury I never had at home. Setting up behind the backstop when your son is playing baseball is another rules violation for player parents. It's a particularly bad idea for a dad who's easily identified by local sports fans. The last thing Sam needed was players and coaches on other teams thinking that his father is some kind of stage dad, browbeating the kid into playing baseball. Remember *Fear Strikes Out*, starring Anthony Perkins as real-life ballplayer Jimmy Piersall? A centerfielder with the Red Sox, Piersall was pressured nonstop by his father and wound up in a mental institution.

The California high schoolers looked good but didn't strike me as far superior to the ballplayers I'd been watching in Massachusetts. They actually looked a little tired. While Newton North was still a week from its season opener, Santa Monica was playing its twenty-fourth game. The Viking players weren't running to their positions at the start of innings—something Sam always did after a coach at one of his baseball camps told him it would make him easier to notice.

Walking back to my hotel in midgame, I struck up a conversation with an elderly man who was wearing an American Legion windbreaker. He was sitting in a big old sedan, parked a respectful three hundred feet from home plate, and he told me he was the grandfather of Santa Monica's cleanup hitter. I'd just seen his grandson whiff on three pitches. He said the boy was a senior and had offers to play baseball at a number of California colleges. For me, this somewhat debunked the alleged mastery of Californian high school baseball players. In the immortal words of Harvard's head coach, I hadn't seen anything special. Then again, we all know a couple of at-bats don't tell you much of anything about any ballplayer.

While in California, I had dinner with Ron Shelton, the former Baltimore Oriole minor leaguer who wrote *Bull Durham*, the best baseball movie ever made (the *New York Times* said it was "about success in failure"). Ron said he was working on a new baseball flick about a Yankee pitcher who has to go to the Mexican League to rediscover his mojo. We talked about baseball traditions and the sanctity of the streak. Shelton captured this beautifully in his epic hardball film, reminding us that baseball is about rituals and respecting streaks. If you think wearing women's underwear will make you a better pitcher, it will make you a better pitcher. Like many hitters, Sam Shaughnessy refuses to wash his uniform while he's enjoying any kind of hitting streak. On an 0-4 day, he'll bring a not-so-dirty uniform to the pantry and stuff it into the washer himself, but when he gets a hit, no detergent can touch the fabric. It can get pretty grimy in humid midsummer, and more than once we've draped Sam's uniform jersey and pants over porch furniture to let fresh air pass through the lucky fibers.

At the end of the month, I got an e-mail from Ilana Miller, a young woman who'd worked for the Red Sox in 2003 when she was a student at the University of Pennsylvania. Ivy-educated, Jewish, and a legitimate young baseball scout, she reminded me of a female Theo Epstein. In her message, she informed me that she'd taken a job as an administrative assistant in the scouting and player development department of the San Diego Padres (where Theo cut his teeth). In closing, she wrote, "I actually saw your son's name in lists of draft-eligible players, but it looks like he's committed to go to school."

The Padres had him on a list. They knew he was going to college. Sam loved that one.

April

THE COWS ALWAYS KNOW.

Growing up in rural Massachusetts, every small child learns that when you see cows lying down in the pasture, rain will follow. I like to think it's because the cows are smart and don't want to trudge through mud.

There were a lot of cows grazing in the grassy fields of Groton and Dunstable in 1971. My backyard featured a mesmerizing view of Gibbet Hill, a grassy slope carved by glaciers and peppered with beautiful Black Angus. Outlined against a blue sky, dotted with livestock, the green hill was a soothing still life framed by the window of our TV room. Not into cow tipping, we steered clear of the Angus when we picnicked in the landing atop the fire tower at the peak of the hill. From that perch, you could see the Prudential Tower in Boston, forty miles to the southeast. The imposing Pru might as well have been the Eiffel Tower for all we cared. In those early years after we got our licenses, none of us dared drive in Boston. We'd dump the car in a parking lot off Route 128 and take the MBTA Riverside car into Fenway Park.

Joanie McGovern, my high school prom date, was a farmer's daughter. Joanie's dad, George McGovern (always a punch line given that this was one year before the 1972 presidential election), had a large dairy farm in the middle of tiny Dunstable. Five of Mr. McGovern's seven children were girls, which makes you somewhat unlucky when you are in the farm business. Those farm girls were tough and hearty, though. Our high school softball team seemed to have a disproportionately high number of players from Dunstable and our primitive data held that the girls from the fields were stronger, harder workers, and therefore better ballplayers. None of them threw like girls, that's for sure.

Joanie's house was seven miles from the middle of Groton, and at 8 A.M. on game days we'd wait for the Dunstable kids to get off the bus and we'd ask about the cows. Horizontal or vertical? Were we going to play baseball later in the day? Or was it going to rain?

Just as I have never seen a taxi in Groton, I'm pretty sure it's been a while since we've had cows in Newton, so we rely on more scientific forecasting in this new century. The Doppler Gang was pretty sure it was going to rain on Friday, April 7, 2006, Newton North's opening day. This was frustrating for me since I'd angled to be home for just about all of Sam's scheduled games. Starting with the Super Bowl in Detroit and ending with the start of the Red Sox season in Texas, I was gone for forty out of sixty-seven nights. It was my plan. I'd covered the Super Bowl, spring training, the World Baseball Classic, and Red Sox Opening Day just so I could be on hand for the games that really mattered—games played by the Newton North Tigers at Howard Ferguson Field.

There were several things I liked about the North squad in 2006. First of all, they had two sets of brothers, and in my experience watching high school sports, the more sets of brothers, the better the team. North had senior captain lefty hurler J. T. Ross and his kid brother Kyle, a sophomore who played three sports fearlessly and was bound for greatness at North. The Tigers also featured Ryan and Mike Walsh, strong, tough kids who could motivate one another as only brothers can. The Tigers squad boasted seven seniors—members of the athletic class who'd already delivered a Super Bowl and a State Champion basketball team. Even better, the roster included nine members of the North Little League where we spent so many weeknights and weekends manning the concession booth and hoping none of the parents would misbehave. One of the seniors on the 2006 North varsity was a kid who perhaps was not good enough to play varsity baseball but was given a uniform because his mom died when he was in high school, and a year later his best friend succumbed to a heart attack. Joe Siciliano knew that you could not cut that boy from the team.

Finally, there was the presence of Ben, a Newton North student afflicted with Down syndrome. Ben was team manager. He took care of the bats and other equipment needs while providing moral support and reminding all of us that even when you go 0-4, you should count your blessings. I loved watching Ben interact with the varsity players. Lots of hugs and pats on the back. Occasionally, he would blurt out, "Come on, Sam, why are you striking out?" but there was always a gentle coach or teammate to remind Ben that only supportive chat is encouraged from folks on your own bench.

North was scheduled to open with Wellesley. The good news for Newton was that Big Nate Freiman was no longer playing for Wellesley. Big Nate was a six foot six pitcher/catcher/slugger who was the best player in our state in his final two years of high school. Sam had worked out with him at the fall clinics at Harvard, and they faced one another in the 2005 season opener when Sam was a junior and Nate was being watched by about fifteen big league scouts. Big Nate threw a one-hitter that day, Sam went 0-3, and it was snowing at the end of the game. Typical season opener in New England. In the end, Big Nate wasn't drafted, but only because all the big league teams knew he was going to Duke.

I was impressed with Nate's folks. They'd had big league scouts coming over to their house and Big Nate pretty much could have gone to any college he wanted, but they rarely mentioned anything about his accomplishments or the hoopla surrounding their talented boy. In the spring of 2006, I got an e-mail from Nate's dad in which he asked about Sam and told me Nate had hurt his elbow and hadn't been able to pitch much for Duke. Len Freiman complimented the Duke coach and medical staff and mentioned that Nate had been able to "finally play against BC last weekend." That was the extent of his description of Nate's performance. I had to go online to learn that Nate was hitting .390 as a freshman in the ACC and had hit three home runs in three games against Boston College. Amazing. Maybe the kid was so good because the parents didn't make a big deal out of his talent.

Watching the season opener in the cold drizzle, I was oddly comfortable nestled into the top-left corner of the aluminum bleachers on the third base side. There couldn't have been more than fifteen or twenty people on hand when the game started. Didn't matter. I'd paid the price and done the time. I'd gone to Los Angeles, Fort Myers, San Diego, Dallas, and a few other warm spots just so I could be in my spot in the top row of those cold metal stands. This was the beginning of the end for Sam and for me. This was where I wanted to be. And in a year, I wouldn't belong there anymore.

Newton led 4–0 in the fourth when we all went home because of rain. Welcome to New England high school baseball.

Sam and I went to see Florida State play at Boston College over the weekend. BC hitters had personalized theme music played when they came to the plate. We heard a lot of Snoop Dogg and other white-guys-trying-to-be-black theme songs, and I asked Sam what he would select when he got to BC.

" 'September' by Earth, Wind & Fire," he said.

Not very intimidating, but very retro.

In the car on the way home, I did the dad thing. More reminders: no drinking. Don't blow it. It's not worth the risk. Don't get caught at some stupid party. I told him the story of the 1986 Celtics, a team of talented, rowdy ballplayers who loved basketball and beer. But Larry Bird, Kevin McHale, Dennis Johnson, Bill Walton, and friends swore off alcohol during the playoffs in 1986 and demolished every team in their path. I suggested that Sam use his captaincy to create a similar team pact.

A couple of days later, Newton beat Wellesley in the "do-over" opener and we went to the Golden Star after the game. I was impressed that Sam wasn't moaning about his error and his hitless performance. He seemed to be getting a better idea of the team concept and the responsibilities of being captain. I had a couple of mai tais while I reminded Sam about not drinking. It struck me that this would be the last year we went to the Chinese restaurant with our kids still wearing their uniforms. It made me a little melancholy—almost enough to order a third mai tai.

The next day was the Red Sox home opener, so I was in the press box at Fenway Park when Newton thrashed Brookline 13–0, a game that was called after only seven innings in accordance with the Bay State League's slaughter rule. Sam's "uncle," Ed Kleven, served as my eyes and ears while I worked at Fenway. Not related by blood, Uncle Eddie has been part of our family since long before Sam was born. Ed grew up in Haverhill, Massachusetts, went to Tufts, and made a career as a rock and roll manager/promoter and later as an agent to athletes and television/radio personalities. He was living in Brookline, next door to the inimitable Peter Gammons, when I first met him in the 1970s. At that time, he represented a dozen or more big league ballplayers. Earlier in his life, he'd been road manager for the Kingsmen ("Louie, Louie") and Dionne Warwick. He'd negotiated with Howard Hughes and George Steinbrenner. Eddie had never married, and he became unofficial uncle to all of our children. If we'd known the Church would have been okay with a Jewish godfather, he'd have stood up at several of our baptisms. Instead, he settled on his status as third parent to our children—ever a go-to guy in an emergency situation. He'd been watching Sam play baseball for a dozen years when I called him from Fenway to learn that Sam got a couple of hits in the rout of Brookline.

The next day I came home from my office at about 2 P.M. and Sam was lying on the coach, watching the Yankees on television. Senior-itis was in full bloom. The local paper, the *Waltham News-Tribune*, was still sitting in front of our house when I pulled up at the curb, and again I was reminded how little Sam and I had in common. He knew there was a story about him in the paper. He knew there was a game account of the Brookline rout. But he couldn't even get his ass off the couch to check out the stories in the paper. Back in the day, if I thought there was a chance of seeing an account of myself playing baseball in the *Public Spirit* pages, I would have been outside the newspaper office at midnight, waiting for the first edition. Then again, I was a guy who'd written *Throw Up for Glory*.

Things bottomed out for our hotshot son a couple of days later when the Tigers beat Xaverian 7–4 on a Saturday morning, the first day of April vacation.

Sam hitting bottom on the day of a big win. Would that be ironic?

Xaverian is a private Catholic high school, with good players from all over eastern Massachusetts. They won the state championship when Sam was a sophomore. The *Boston Herald* highlighted this game as "one to watch" in its preseason roundup, and the star scholastic reporter Danny Ventura was in the stands to see James Greeley dazzle the X-Men over six innings while Newton pounded out fourteen hits for a third straight victory.

But there was no seat at the table for Sam in this feast. He went 0-2 with a couple of walks. He looked lazy chasing an errant pickoff throw. He also threw his helmet after popping up with two men aboard, and he didn't seem engaged on the bench when his teammates were standing and cheering during Newton's rallies. He was pouting. When the game was over, I noticed he was sent out to drag the infield with one of the underclassmen. Not a typical chore for a senior captain.

After the game, Marilou and I went to lunch with Kate and her boyfriend. This was Kate's junior year at Boston University, and she'd retired from the college softball team and was spending part of her spring semester as coach of the freshman softball team at Newton North. She has great respect for the game and understands the plight of those less gifted, those who sometimes linger on the end of the bench. Kate was a first-team Bay State League All-Star at North, but the BU coaches never gave her a chance after she made the team as a walk-on for the first two seasons of her college life. She was allowed only one at-bat in two years, about a hundred games (grounded to the infield). In her exit interview, she told the coach she'd never do that to a player—there's always a spot to get kids in, even at the Division I level with a team of scholarship athletes. Now she was putting that pledge into play with the thirteen Newton North girls who were not good enough to make the varsity or junior varsity as freshmen. I loved watching Kate cajole her Bad News Bear cubs. Hers was a roster peppered with players from the Lake area —Italian girls with giant walls of hair and names like Pelligrini and DeNucci. They lost their opener 17–2.

Kate's status as a coach put her inside the loop at the North athletic department, and as she arrived at lunch she informed me that there was a scene involving Sam and Coach Siciliano earlier that day, before the Xaverian game. Sam had arrived five minutes before he was to report, then went about his business eating a sausage and cheese bagel from Dunkin' Donuts while

Sis was addressing the team. He got into a jam with a teammate over something stupid involving the other guy's equipment. This came on the heels of Sam's week of half-assed practices, low-lighted when he neglected to slide during a scrimmage, which forced the entire team to do sliding drills. Sis snapped. He took Sam to the side and screamed at him. Assistant Coach Tom Donnellan steered the rest of the team away from the scene.

Sis told Sam he was a lousy teammate. He told him he was no longer a captain. At the end, he told Sam not to talk about it with any of his teammates. Just shut up and play. Naturally, Sam did the opposite and tried to galvanize his teammates against their coach. More ugly conversations.

Hearing Kate relay all this made me sick to my stomach. I left my half-eaten omelet on the table and went home to find Sam.

He was lying on the couch, watching the Red Sox. I told him to turn off the TV, then asked him to explain himself. He asked what I had heard, but I wasn't giving it up. This was bad. I'd done my best to show him the way, but he'd turned into the kind of entitled, spoiled athlete that I'd regularly ripped.

After much argument and attempts to portray himself as a victim, I got Sam to admit, "Okay, I ate a bagel and I didn't slide! I'm a terrible person!"

I wasn't having it. This was ridiculous. Embarrassed, I called Coach Siciliano. He said to come on over.

The drive was pretty quiet.

"This is it, Sam," I said. "You apologize and ask Coach what you need to do to make things right. Stop playing the victim. You want to blow this whole thing now? Go ahead. People your age are fighting wars and I'm going with you to see your high school coach? Not anymore. You decide. Next year at BC, they won't be talking to your dad. They'll throw your ass off the team. And you can go get a job. I'm not bankrolling this venture anymore if my kid is going to be the asshole."

It was the first time I'd been to Coach Siciliano's house. I asked if he wanted me to stay or if he wanted to work things out with Sam alone. He asked me to stay. The three of us sat at his kitchen table, Sam in the middle, chair angled to face his coach.

I didn't plan on saying much but figured for starters Sam should apologize. I started to say, "Sam has something he wants to say to you," but didn't get the whole sentence out.

"No," said the coach, still wearing a Newton ball cap, black team turtleneck, and warm-up jacket. "I don't want apologies. I want Sam to explain why he's been acting this way this week. I want him to tell me if I've been getting his best effort at practice. I want to know why it's so hard for him to be a captain. I want to know why he can't be more supportive of his teammates. I want to know why he didn't move his feet on that throw to first today. I want to know why he doesn't wear his cup to practice when everybody else does. Why he wears sweats when everybody else wears baseball pants. Why he wears a BC sweatshirt when everybody else is wearing Newton North jackets. And I don't want him to tell me it's just Sam being Sam. Tom Donnellan and I went to breakfast at the Knotty Pine at seven A.M. today, and I told Tom I was planning to talk to Sam about all this after today's game. Then he shows up and he's eating when I'm talking and then he gets into it with Walsh. What's going on, Sam? You have to ask yourself why you are doing this."

Sam didn't have much to say. He admitted he wasn't going all out in practice. He said the dust-up with his teammate had started out as a joke. He said it was hard for him to support his teammates when he wasn't contributing himself.

"I just get frustrated," he said.

"Sam, I know you're not comfortable with being a captain," said Siciliano. "But if we're going to win a state championship, you being a captain gives us a better chance. You need to be one of the senior leaders. We've been doing this for four years."

God bless Sis. He gave Sam another chance. He was angry that Sam had talked to players about having his captaincy stripped, but he figured out a way around the problem.

"In two weeks, Sam, I'm going to call the team together after a win. I'm going to say, 'Sam and I had a problem. But we worked on it. Some of you may have been told he lost his captaincy. What do you guys think? Should Sam be a captain?' We'll leave it up to your teammates."

It was more than fair. Sam was on probation. It was up to him to patch things with his teammates. And they would get to pass judgment on his new efforts.

Coach and Sam shook hands and agreed on this course of action. I said little. Then Sis said, "I'm looking forward to the game against Waltham Monday morning [vacation week]."

I asked Coach what time Sam was to be at the field. He said 9:30. Then Sam said, "Want me to meet you and Tom at the Knotty Pine at seven?"

We thanked Sis and were on our way. I told Sam I didn't want to talk about it anymore, except to say that I knew he wasn't wild about being a captain, but the idea of losing the title in this manner was unacceptable. I reminded him that at the high school level, the best players are always captain. If not, it usually means the kid is a jerk.

"Think of how it would have looked if Gurley hadn't been captain of basketball, or if Big Nate hadn't been captain at Wellesley last year. You'd wonder what was wrong with the kid."

In my view, he had shamed the entire family, tainted some of the good work done by his sisters years before him. I followed four older siblings to Groton High School and more was expected of me because of what they had done there. More was given, too. It was easier for me because of the high school lives they had lived. Same for Sam. Teachers and coaches loved his sisters, and that was a reflection of his parents, too. Now he was undoing some of their good work. Going back in time, I know what would have been the reaction of Bemis Bag sales engineer Bill Shaughnessy. He never would have known what happened because he was not a hands-on sports parent like me and he didn't have moles at the school like I had in Kate. But had he ever learned of such a transgression, it would have been the end of baseball for me. And there would not have been a lot of discussion about it. *"Too late, Danny. I don't think we need baseball for you anymore."*

Back in 1971, the feisty Albane knew how to be a good teammate. Nobody got more frustrated than Al. He was a talented athlete but somewhat miscast on a baseball diamond. We used to call him "shortstop without a glove," as in "sheriff without a gun," because he seemed to be able to field the position without using any leather. He'd let ground balls bounce off his chest, pick them up, and throw out the runner. At home plate, he took Reggie Jacksonesque cuts at just about every pitch, and when he went down swinging, it was like watching a mechanized corkscrew go into the top of a wine bottle. But he didn't take the game, or himself, too seriously. In the spring of 1971, we had a flossy sophomore infielder, Bobby Perreault, who clearly was going to be an outstanding player in a year or two, but struggled when he faced varsity pitching for the first time. In April, when Bobby was in the throes of a monster slump, Albane performed one of his grunt-filled, dust-swirling strikeouts, walked back to our bench, sat down next to Bobby, turned to the kid, and said, "I hope you know I did that just to make you feel good!"

Now that's what I call leadership.

Sam and I went to Fenway on Easter Sunday, the day after he'd lost his "C." He knew I was pissed. Little was said in the car on the way to the ballpark. He took the bus home alone while I worked. We had a family dinner that night, and Sam was dispatched to Harvard Stadium to pick up Sarah, who was coming in on a bus back from New Haven. She'd gotten a pinch hit against Yale and was hitting .375 (3-8) in limited duty. I loved that. Sam's sister was playing D-I softball and she was outhitting her big-shot, bad-boy brother. I broke his chops about it a few times while we were breaking bread.

The next day was Marathon Monday, and the Newton Tigers were home for the fourth straight game. The game started at eleven. Sam was there a couple of hours early.

Howard L. Ferguson Field is a fairly typical high school baseball field. It's about 340 feet down the line in both directions and it abuts a lacrosse field on one side and tennis courts on the other. When a pop-up drifts out of play on the first base side, those playing tennis are always at risk. The baseball players have taken to yelling "Tennis!" whenever a ball is bound for the hard courts, and the tennis players respond by holding their racquets over their heads. Incredibly, in four years of watching dozens of fouls plop onto the courts, I have never seen a tennis player hit by a baseball.

Newton beat Waltham 4–0 on Patriots Day. Sam hit an RBI double and appeared to be engaged with his teammates. Sis called that night and told me, "It was a 180-degree turnaround. I wish I could address that captain thing right now, but I'd better wait a couple of days."

I thanked him and told him I'd appreciated how he'd handled Sam at the meeting at his house.

"Glad to hear you say that," the coach said. "I was afraid you were going to be mad at me."

When I heard him say that, I realized that in 2006, a coach of a high school team no doubt routinely has parents rushing to the defense of their children after punishment is handed out. Baby boomer parents take their job seriously and a misbehaving kid can be a commentary on the quality of home instruction. Therefore, coaches who sanction ballplayers often incur the wrath of Mom or Dad. It couldn't possibly be junior's fault.

Not me. I know my kids, and I like to think I can read the intent of veteran schoolteachers and coaches. It has rarely been my instinct to defend Sam when I'm told he's screwing up. If that makes Sam feel like he's not being backed up, too bad. He's going to have teachers and bosses that he doesn't like—maybe even a tough father-in-law. God forbid he ever had to serve in the armed forces, where folks with higher ranks sometimes abuse those under their command just for the sport of it. Our kids have to learn to get along with the authority figures, and watching Mom and Dad blame the coach sends a terrible message.

Vacation week was uneventful, thank God. No 3 A.M. taxis. No late night phone calls. No more complaints from teachers or coaches. Sam would yell upstairs when he came home after midnight. Some nights I was already asleep and didn't hear him, but when I got up for the nightly old-man trip to pee at 3 A.M., I'd look out the window and feel a sense of relief when I saw the hunter-green Acura in the driveway. He was home, downstairs, in bed. Whew.

As we held our breath en route to the finish line, I remembered the incredible independence I'd been granted in the spring of my senior year. I cracked open the ancient diary and there it was: on Friday, May 7, 1971, my parents left for Germany, turning over the house to their 17-year-old high school senior. I'd like to say the freedom resulted in some kind of *Risky Business* wildness, but in truth, there were no parties at our home on Hollis Street, and I was never tempted to break into Mom and Dad's liquor cabinet, where a bottle of Seagram's stood next to half-gallons of Chardonnay. Dad's cans of Miller High Life, which he drank only when watching the Red Sox after doing lawn work, also went untouched. The ever-cooler-than-me Heather Stoddart visited a couple of times, but the big event was when she made me a TV dinner. It was nothing like Tom Cruise and Rebecca De Mornay, and there was no Ivy League representative to eventually tell my dad, "Princeton can use a guy like Danny." Sure, I invited the guys over a couple of times, but our pathetic, innocent fun primarily consisted of watching the Red Sox, then staying up late for Johnny Carson. I went to school every day, played base-ball every afternoon, and kept track of my batting average, just as Sam would thirty-five years later. I worked my shifts at John-son's and watched the Sox (in black and white) whenever they were on TV. Good thing there was no *SportsCenter* in those days. It would have been hard to get any work done.

The idea of leaving Sam by himself at home for two weeks —especially in the spring of his senior year—was unthinkable.

Sam hosted a team dinner the night before the Tigers played Walpole at the end of vacation week. It was the ultimate boy bonding event—barbeque, Red Sox on the plasma, and no par-ents. The definition of lame would be parents who hang around during a high school team dinner. It's especially creepy if you are a dad and your daughter has the softball team over for grub. Middle-aged men are invisible to teenage girls, and there is noth-ing any dad can say or do that will make him appear cool. Any attempt at coolness is guaranteed to embarrass his daughter. Bet-ter to make yourself scarce. This was easily accomplished in April 2006 because Marilou and I were both working the night Sam invited his teammates to eat. Kate stopped by and made sure the boys didn't blow up the house with the propane grill, and when the last of the teammates left, Sam looked at his mom—who had just gotten home from work—and said, "That went well." He'd even cleaned up. What a guy. I saw it as another step toward eras-ing the disgrace of his lost captaincy.

Newton North suffered its first loss the next day. Sam struck out twice and walked three times and was putting his uniform in the washing machine before the sun went down. A quarter of the season was gone, and he was hitting .214 (3-14) with a whopping nine walks in five games. The good news was that the team was winning and he didn't seem to be pressing. A year ear-

lier, this would have been a disaster, because he'd have been worried about his statistics and impressing the college coaches and
scouts.

I went to bed after midnight on the last Saturday of Sam's vacation and when I got up for the nightly 3 A.M. trip to the bathroom, I noticed no Acura in the driveway. I went downstairs and
Sam's bed was empty.

"He was here at one in the morning when I went to bed,"
Marilou offered as I woke her with the news.

She called his cell.

"Sam, where are you? . . . Can you come right home?"

She hung up the phone and said, "He said he's driving around."

I left Marilou in the kitchen to wait for our son. She'd been
the specialist for these post-midnight confessions.

Sam came into the house a few minutes later and I did my
best to listen from my third-floor nest.

"I just needed to get some fresh air," he said, sounding completely sober and measured. "When I'm not doing good in baseball, it feels like nothing else is going right. It's frustrating for me.
Right now, I just want senior year to be over. Everything seems
stupid. I just want to get on to BC."

They talked for an hour and a half, winding up on the second
floor, where Sam played his mom some of his favorite music. He
was still into anything by Warren Zevon ("My Ride's Here" was a
new favorite) and Cat Stevens's "Sad Lisa."

Sam went to bed at 5 A.M. and slept until one in the afternoon. He was working on a new stance when I finally saw him
vertical again.

"I've been landing on my front foot too soon," he said. "I
think that's why I haven't been swinging so much. It's probably
going to be a while until I start hitting now that I'm using this
new stance."

There is such a thing as a prescription for failure. You can even make your excuses ahead of time. Sam was setting himself up, and sure enough, on the first day back from vacation he went 0-4 with three strikeouts in a victory over Framingham. I could hardly believe my eyes. He took five pitches in his first at-bat, swinging at none, and getting called out on strikes. After a harmless fly to center, he went up two more times and struck out awkwardly both times. The big-shot, D-I recruit was failing miserably. It reminded me of his freshman year, when he was called up to varsity and struggled against the older kids. He went 4-22 that year, with a whopping twelve strikeouts. Now he was the oldest kid and had the big reputation, and he was doing even worse. He had willed himself into a slump.

"Well, that was kind of rough," I said when he got into the car after the game (Kate was using a car for her softball team, so Sam was riding with his parents again, and this seemed somehow to be contributing to his return to freshman year in every way).

"I'm 1-14 with five strikeouts in my last four games," he said.

"Sam, we've been over this. You've talked yourself into this. You've got to stop worrying about stats and awards. Just forget all that and be a team guy. I know it's hard for you, but the team is winning and you're doing nothing. Think of how good you guys will be when you start to hit. And you will hit. You don't lose it overnight. This seems like a lot, but it's a small sampling. A few games. And until today, you didn't really look bad. Stop thinking about it so much. Try to remember what it is you love about the game—how much you love hitting—and it'll come back to you."

We didn't talk much after that. I left him alone, except to offer to watch a *Twilight Zone* episode with him while he ate dinner. He was going to have to figure this out on his own. But it was tearing me up, too. There's an old expression that a parent is only as happy as his or her saddest child, and I knew we had one unhappy guy living in Teenage Wasteland. It's completely stupid and trivial in the scheme of life, but five strikeouts in two days and a

.166 batting average (3-18) can do that when your whole world is baseball. I reminded myself not to tease Sam anymore about getting outslugged by his Harvard sister. He didn't need that.

Sam was surprisingly calm the next couple of days. Humbled, even. Perhaps it was Buddha. He helped his mother clean the basement without complaint. He didn't bitch and moan about not having any wheels while Kate used the Acura to commute to her softball practices from Boston University. He didn't even bother to wash his uniform. The hitless white number 24 just lay there on the floor of his junky room. I couldn't figure out whether Sam had taken my advice or just given up.

Two days after the disastrous game, Newton traveled to Norwood for its first road game of the season. It was cold and windy and the game was played on top of a hill that had a graveyard behind the backstop. Ball yards and bone yards are often aligned. Happy sounds for eternal rest, no?

Sam snapped out of it against Norwood with a couple of hits. He was locked in again. And he was smiling. After the game, before Sam boarded the team bus, I told him to meet me at the Golden Star for dinner and to bring as many teammates as he wanted.

An hour later, Big Nick Wolfe and Sam, dirty and sweating, still wearing their white uniforms with the orange and black trim, joined me in our traditional corner booth at the Star. When Marilou arrived from work, we had a foursome. We rehashed the game, talked about Newton's extraordinary pitching, and the boys informed us that they already had prom dates. Softball second baseman, Emily, Sam's stunning date from junior year, had asked him to the senior prom. He said he'd be needing a tux. Kate later suggested the orange model that Jim Carrey wore in *Dumb and Dumber*.

The dark, dank Star was always good for these kinds of moments. We'd been going there since before any of the kids were born, and a lot of family folklore unfolded in the corner booth.

We'd had discussions about figure skating, summer family trips, Kate's cancer treatment, the merits of *Titanic,* SAT prep, and coaches who didn't let all the kids play. Birthdays and anniversaries were celebrated there, and usually we had kids still in uniform. That's why it was such a blow when I went to use the phone booth in the gloomy barroom and one of the regulars told me, "This place is closing Sunday."

Shocking, but true. I confirmed it with Vinnie, one of the Chinese owners. Due to a lease issue, they were shutting down on Sunday night, April 30. The bar regulars were already planning a Friday night wake. A couple of them jokingly (I think) said they were planning an occupation, which had been done with some success recently by loyal parishioners who refused to leave their churches after they were scheduled to be closed by the archdioceses.

For the Shaughnessys, news that the Star was closing was like the death of a family pet. The Star was part of our history. We were losing a place where we had gathered, a place where *things had happened.* Given that traditional family dinners hardly exist in our time, it's not an exaggeration to say that the Shaughnessys had almost as many all-inclusive family dinners at the Star than we had in our house in the eighteen years since Sam rounded out the clan.

Sam called Sarah on her cell phone to tell his sister the bad news.

"No fucking way!" we heard as Sam pulled the phone away from his ear.

"Sarah, language!" said Marilou.

Kate was similarly outraged and saddened. We made plans to return to the Star repeatedly for the final four days. We planned to ask Vinnie about buying some dishes or other Star mementos. Kate suggested we take home the corner booth and have clinical psychologist Dr. Marilou Shaughnessy use it for the waiting area of her soon-to-be-built home office.

Hmmm. Interesting idea. We could re-create our family booth from the Golden Star—sort of like Kramer assembling the set of the *Merv Griffin Show* in his Manhattan apartment.

A few days later, North played Braintree, the same team they'd beaten one year earlier on Sam's walkoff homer the day of Michael's wake. The Tigers won again, beating the Wamps (love those New England Indian names) 7–3. Sam went 2-3 with a double and two more walks. He was up to .304 from .166 in just two games. He was back and he hadn't even washed his uniform.

We went to the Golden Star after the Braintree game and again every night until it closed. After rediscovering his stroke, Sam discovered scallion pancakes.

The closing of the Star was a neighborhood event. Patrons took photos in front of the place, and the Newton police sent a sheet cake, thanking the owners for forty years of great service and free meals. The last day of the month was the last night at the Star, Sunday, April 30. I picked up Sarah at school while Kate and Sam delivered uncle Eddie so he could have one more dish of his favorite Chicago chicken chow mein. Marilou was in Detroit, visiting her dad on his eightieth birthday, and we teased her about skewed priorities. Dads turn 80 every day, but the closing of the Star happens only once.

Vinnie had our circular booth waiting when we got there, and Kate took a million photos as we went through the paces of our family routine one last time. Along with the post-meal pineapple and fortune cookies, Vinnie gave us a doggie bag filled with Golden Star menus, mai tai glasses, scorpion bowls, and a duck sauce cup.

Walking out the front door of the Golden Star for the last time, posing for a photo in front of the big yellow sign, I realized this was both a passage and a harbinger. This is what I was going to feel like when Sam played his last game of high school ball. It was happening too fast and I wasn't ready yet.

May

BASEBALL AMERICA and Perfect Game, reputable organizations of amateur baseball scouting, released a ranking of the top fifteen high school players in Massachusetts, and Sam was listed fourth. At the same time, the *Boston Globe* listed the pitching-powered Newton North Tigers as the fourth-best team in eastern Massachusetts, Sam was back up over .300, and it looked like it was going be a fun ride to the state tournament.

And then I saw Sam throw his bat while he was still in the batter's box after getting called out on strikes.

On May Day.

Monday, May 1, was another truly horrible spring day, the kind that sometimes makes New Englanders ask themselves, "Why do we live here?" There seemed to be a lot of these in 2006. The Red Sox were preparing to play host to the Yankees for the first time all season and frosty, tarp-covered Fenway was bracing for the return of Johnny Damon. The bearded, shaggy-haired face of the 2004 champion Red Sox, Damon had permanently tarnished his reputation in Boston by taking Yankee money in the off season of 2005–2006. He went from Jesus to Judas with one stroke of a pinstriped pen.

In 1992, when he was a senior at Dr. Phillips High School in

Orlando, Damon had been rated the top high school baseball prospect in the country. At a perfectly sculpted six foot two and 190 pounds, he had speed, power, aggressiveness, and good baseball makeup. He played hard but didn't smash helmets when he made outs. It was all natural. And he didn't have his dad spending money to show him off to college coaches and pro scouts. Johnny's parents barely knew about his athletic gifts. Sergeant Jimmy Damon was an American serviceman from Illinois who met his bride in Thailand. When Johnny was playing his high school ball in Florida, both of his parents were working two jobs. Johnny's folks got somewhat annoyed when those college coaches and pro scouts started calling the house during his senior year. The folks hadn't really seem him play and didn't know what all the fuss was about until the Kansas City Royals drafted him in the first round and paid him a bonus of $250,000 to report to the Gulf Coast League. Fourteen years later, Damon came back to Fenway Park, a traitor superstar with a $52 million contract.

J. T. Ross got the start at Walpole on May 1, and it was clear that this was going to be a pitcher's day. It was about 42 degrees and the wind was whipping toward home plate. Parents froze as a succession of hitters from both teams trudged back to the dugout after whiffing. Sam had been hit by a pitch and struck out when walked to the plate to face a hard-throwing Walpole lefty who was painting both corners. Sam worked the count to 3-1, then took a pitch that appeared to be high and away. But umpires get cold, too, and every hitter needs to expand his strike zone when the weather sucks.

"Strike two!"

Frustrated, Sam committed a cardinal sin of sports: he allowed a questionable call to impact his next moment. And it was obvious that he was still stewing over the 3-1 pitch when he looked at the next one, which was right down the middle.

Rightfully rung up, but still convinced he'd been wronged,

Sam wheeled out of the box, raised his bat over his shoulder with his left arm, and spiked it into the ground in the direction of his own team's bench on the first base side. It did not go near anyone, but had it slipped out of his hand, it could have hit one of his teammates or coaches. Equally bad, he'd shown up the umpire with this demonstration. A coach and a couple of players on the Walpole side objected briefly, but no one else said much of anything as Sam stalked toward his bench, picked up his useless bat, set it down where it belonged, and sat.

Had I been working behind the plate, I'd have ejected him.

The whole day went pretty much like that. Newton had a run taken off the board when it was ruled that a base runner left too early on a sac fly and lost 2–1 in eleven innings. Sam whiffed three times and left several in scoring position. Ross, emerging as one of the best pitchers in the state, struck out fourteen.

After the game, I drove to Fenway like a madman and called Sam from the press box after the boos rained down on Johnny Damon.

"Sam—the bat," I started.

"I know, I know. I apologized to Sis. I apologized to the ump."

"Don't give me 'I know, I know.' This cannot keep happening. Word gets around. This has to stop."

We never talked about it again. I was worn out and giving up. As a baseball lifer, I'm ever mindful of how the game should be played. One has to respect the game and play by its rules, written and unwritten. Seeing Sam repeatedly violate the tenets of the game depressed and discouraged me. He was at times the personification of that which was wrong with today's game. It hurt and embarrassed me that he hadn't learned better, that he couldn't put the essence of the game ahead of his own self interests. At times like this, I reminded myself that Sam was going to have to figure it out on his own, or just stop playing baseball.

The humbled Tigers enjoyed a couple of blowouts when the weather turned summerlike later in that week. They slaughtered Weymouth and Needham. I felt bad for the Needham kids. One of their teammates had committed suicide in April. The Needham players had his number 5 on the backs of the game day hats and several had served as pallbearers. It was going to be a long, gloomy spring for the Rockets.

Late in the Friday afternoon blowout against Needham, Sam stepped to the plate for his final at-bat of the day and got drilled in the right foot with the first pitch. You could hear it from the parking lot. He wheeled out of the box, filled the air with a non-expletive (*"ARRRRRGGGGG"*), and slammed his bat into the ground. No crime against baseball there. It was a standard response from one who'd been hit in the bone with a fastball. Clearly in pain, he limped down the line, then came out for a pinch runner. The customary high school ice bag was produced from the standard high school medical kit. After the game, Assistant Coach Tom Donnellan recommended that Sam get the foot x-rayed. Running around with a cracked bone in one's foot is guaranteed to sabotage a promising athletic career.

Even though it would have meant the end of his high school year—just when the mighty Tigers were enjoying their best season in twenty years—Sam wasn't worried about a potential broken bone. High school kids believe they are athletically bulletproof. It has always astounded me how few of them actually do get hurt. Three-sport stars throw their bodies into two-way football, then live to play basketball and baseball without missing a game. In my sophomore and junior years of high school basketball, we had the same five players start every game. Two years. No broken bones. No torn ACLs. Not even a bad case of the flu. Infinite good health: it is something we take for granted in our teens.

Seeing Sam hit the deck and grimace in pain reminded me

how fragile all this is. I pondered the possibility that this was it. What a way to finish. The Golden Star, then Sam, both shut down in the same week.

At ten the next morning we drove to St. Elizabeth's Hospital, where Dr. Bill Morgan had agreed to meet us and give Sam a quick x-ray. This was a big favor. I'd befriended Morgan when he was medical director of the Red Sox. Sox management had since replaced him, but he still ran one of the top orthopedic clinics in New England. Sam was going to get an instant analysis from the same guy who stitched a dead man's body parts into the ankle of Curt Schilling to get Big Schill on the mound for those two bloody sock games in October 2004.

Funny, but I don't recall getting any personal treatment from the Red Sox team doctor when I cut off the tip of my thumb while making coleslaw with an electric slicer at Johnson's Drive-In during my senior year.

Dr. Morgan met us in the lobby, took us upstairs, and within seconds was looking at live video of Sam's skeletal foot. Great news. No break. He told Sam he'd be able to play on Monday.

"Pretty good," Sam said as we walked to the car. "It was especially cool that he was wearing his championship ring."

We went to breakfast to celebrate the unbroken foot. Sam devoured a bacon and cheese omelet, half a loaf of bread, *and* a side order of French toast, all washed down with a Coke.

"He's like a dog," Sam's mom noted when I replayed the breakfast menu. "He wolfs down a ton of food in a matter of minutes, but he only eats once a day."

Sam went to practice that afternoon but didn't run or put any weight on the foot yet. After the game, the entire team walked over to the girls' softball field to cheer for their classmates at the annual Newton North versus Newton South softball game. Good tradition. Good camaraderie. It's somewhat standard to see the kids coming together in the last days of high school. In 1971, our class of gypsies, tramps, thieves, and abject losers totally bonded as we neared graduation. Cliques broke down, and we stopped making fun of the kid with the white socks and the bad complexion. The reality of the finality washed over us and brought us together. The small stuff, the pettiness born of our own insecurities, ceased to matter anymore. There were kids I'd hardly ever spoken with, kids I'd shared corridor space with for twelve or thirteen years . . . and only at the end did I make an effort to know them; only when it was almost over and I knew I'd probably never see them again.

In mid-May, Jonathan Holmes, one of those classmates from 1971, asked me to come back to Groton to speak to the 2006 Groton-Dunstable Regional High School senior athletes at the old Groton Country Club. Jon had a senior daughter on the basketball team and he was involved with an athletic Boosters Club, which certainly didn't exist when we were in high school. The old Country Club *was* around in my day, however, and I had some serious flashbacks as I pulled into the parking lot by the first-hole tees. This was where my sister's wedding reception was held in 1967 when I had to miss that Babe Ruth playoff game. This was where the grownups held the infamous "country club dances," semiformal events where a few handpicked "town" kids got to mingle with the private school snobs who always seemed to have better skin than we did (Stephen Stills's "Change Partners" covers it nicely). The Country Club was also the training site for our cross-country teams, and it was on the second and third holes of the course that I'd staggered up those ski slope hills, wheezing and gasping with every step. As kids we'd waded into the golf course's water traps to score Titleists that we'd later hit out of our hands with baseball bats. Hit a golf ball square with the barrel of a Louisville Slugger and for that moment you knew what if felt like to be Mickey Mantle. I could hit those suckers clear over my neighbor's red barn, halfway to the tower atop Gibbet Hill.

The Groton Country Club was also the site of our junior and senior proms, and our 1971 Senior Bash. The Senior Bash was an overnight event, produced and promoted by our parents, and held the night before commencement. The idea was to keep us out of trouble in those final dark hours before they officially cut us loose. After the diplomas we'd be on our own, but before graduation we were still under the watch of our parents and teachers. The Bash went from 8 P.M. until 4 A.M., where we drank cola, danced, signed yearbooks, made out, and slept in corners of the dark country club ballroom. One of our classmates, Rod Smith, was not there on the night of our grand farewell. Rod was a kid who rarely said anything and once wore the same red shirt to school for twenty-three consecutive days. In our yearbook, he'd bragged about never having attended a single after-school activity in four years of high school. Full of our own insecurity, we'd made fun of him behind his back, but we had only ninety-one seniors in our class and we wanted him there for the Senior Bash, so we got some of our prettiest girls to call him on a country club pay phone. They begged him to attend but had no luck. Rod kept his record intact while the rest of us finally got to know one another—the way people stuck in an elevator might get to know one another. At 4 A.M., we caravanned to the high school, where our parents made us breakfast. Then we went home to bed. By the time we got up the next afternoon, it was just about time for graduation ceremonies.

In early May 2006, parents of Newton North seniors received a letter from the cochairs of "Celebration 2006," the all-night party slated to be held after the prom. Making no attempt to veil the message, the missive stated, "The underlying reason for having the party is to keep our young people safe on a night that is historically perilous for prom-goers."

The Shaughnessy family had been lucky regarding prom-night problems. More than broken hearts or drunken driving, it was state softball tournament conflicts that had topped our list of troubles. The better your team was, the more likely you'd end up with a tournament game on the same day as prom night. Early in the twenty-first century, the Newton North softball coach Lauren Baugher was not too happy when a couple of her players elected to get their hair done *before* a state tournament game because they wouldn't have time to do it after the game on the way to the celebrity ball. I'll not soon forget the image of softball players sitting on the bench with crowns of perfectly styled curls piled atop their heads. Try squashing a size 7¼ batting helmet over that. Not pretty.

Looking ahead in '06, the Newton North Tigers figured to be playing their first tournament game around June 1. The prom was June 5, graduation was June 7, and the state tourney didn't end until June 17. Good thing Sam didn't have to worry about getting his hair done.

The Tigers stopped hitting and came back to earth with a couple of losses in the rain-soaked second week of May. Big Nick Wolfe extended his season-long scoreless inning streak to thirty-three innings before giving up a pair of runs in the Brookline game, which was played at the home field of Northeastern University in Brookline. Sam was up to .325 by the end of the week but only had four extra base hits and zero homers through the first thirteen games of the season. Those bats I'd brought back from Florida were hardly looking like weapons of mass destruction. I remember Derek Lowe once telling me, "I hit .500 in high school, but doesn't everybody hit .500 in high school?" Not in the cold, rainy, Bay State League in 2006.

In the midst of more carwash rains on Mother's Day weekend, Sam went to City Sports to buy new batting gloves. Reluctantly, I gave him some cash.

"No more called third strikes," I urged. "If I'm paying for batting gloves, I want my money's worth. Swing the goddamn bat!"

He laughed. Sort of.

When the new *Globe* rankings came out in the middle of the month, the 9-4 Tigers had slipped to number ten. They'd lost four games by a total of five runs and, like every other team in the state, they were facing a lot of games in a short amount of time if the rain ever stopped.

This was no ordinary rainfall. It was historic. It was biblical. No one had ever seen anything like it. In a period of three days, greater Boston received more than a foot of rain, and by the fifteenth of the month it was already the second-wettest May in more than one hundred years of record-keeping. It was the worst local flooding in seventy years. Roads were closed. Schools were closed. A state of emergency was declared, rivers overflowed, and there were fears that dams might burst. Some North Shore towns canceled school for three straight days. People were evacuated and lives were endangered. Senators Kerry and Kennedy sought federal relief funds. We went eight days without seeing the sun. It was a true local crisis.

And all I could think about was how the rain was screwing up Joe Siciliano's pitching rotation. And what was this going to do to the state tournament? Some of the fields on the North Shore were under several feet of water. Would all the games ever be made up?

Newton North returned to the field in Braintree on Wednesday night, May 17. It was the Tigers' first game in seven days, and it was played under the lights in an effort to give the Braintree grass an extra three hours to dry.

Dear old dad got a little nostalgic making that final trip to Braintree. How many times had I been down those roads? Sarah scored her first field hockey goal in Braintree. I saw it from a window in a stairwell outside the Braintree gym, where Kate was playing a volleyball match at the same time as her sister's field hockey game. I'd seen Sam play freshman football on the Braintree gridiron, and our girls had engaged in vicious competition with the Wamp softball team on the same sprawling complex. North's basketball team always considered the Braintree players dirty and when Sam got ejected for breaking a kid's nose in a junior varsity scrum, he was privately applauded by the Newton basketball staff. It was the only time they were glad his temper got the best of him. A bustling town south of Boston, Braintree is one of the more inconvenient outposts in the Bay State League, and many a time I'd gotten trapped in early rush hour traffic while barreling down the Southeast Expressway toward a softball or baseball game. I'd also gotten lost a few times, but not in May 2006. By this time I could have given tours of Braintree, and the various sub shops and doughnut stores en route to the ball fields. It made me a little sad to be driving there for the last time as a parent of a Newton North ballplayer.

I had a pretty good idea which Newton parents would make the same trip through traffic. Ed Lee, father of our sure-handed second baseman, Alex, never missed a game. He'd played college baseball and ran many of the summer and winter baseball programs for the kids. He knew a lot about equipment and had furnished Sam with a first baseman's mitt for the 2006 season. Cheryl Cosmo would be there. Her son, James Greeley, had pitched in just about every game. Cheryl was famous for stalking the premises, talking on her cell phone, and fighting the inner battle that plagues every pitcher's mom and dad. She found it difficult to stay calm, and every time I looked up she'd be in another corner of the ballpark, pacing. Meg and Mark Ross were season-ticket holders, home and away. They had two boys starting for North and it wouldn't be an official game if we didn't hear Meg belting out, "Come on, J. T., little poke!" a couple of times in the course of nine innings. Larry Amato, dad of our shortstop, paced and chatted, went to the woods for a smoke, and admitted he was a Yankee fan. Catcher Ryan Mac's dad was a cop and never said much of anything. Third baseman Ryan

Walsh's dad was similarly stoic and his mom was habitually late, but I'm pretty sure their presence meant something to the boys. The idea that parents existed who never saw their kids play completely amazed me. I realize not everybody can alter their work schedule to watch high school sports, but what could be more fulfilling than sitting in the last row of the bleachers by yourself and watching your son play high school baseball? Eighteen holes of golf? Please.

That soggy night in Braintree turned out to be a breakout game for Sam. In a 10–5 victory over the Wamps, he walked twice, scored four runs, and went 3-3, including an eighth-inning grand slam over the 360 sign in center. Ever surgical at home plate, he swung at only four of the twenty-one pitches thrown to him. The Tigers clinched a spot in the state tourney with their tenth victory, but there was a big loss when Nicky Wolfe injured his knee running the bases in the first inning. He went for x-rays that night, and it looked like he might be done for the season.

Nicky was on crutches the next day when the Tigers lost to Dedham 5–1. Dedham featured a big righthanded pitcher, Holy Cross–bound Bobby Holmes, who stopped our Tigers on one run in six-plus innings and also hit a home run. While Holmes was demonstrating that he was the best player in the Bay State League, Peter Gammons was on the radio telling people that Sam was going to be selected in the major league draft in June. A national baseball icon and legitimate Hall of Famer, Peter is also a good Groton boy who grew up playing baseball with Bill Shaughnessy. Peter's prediction seemed preposterous, especially given Sam's 2006 high school performance in comparison to some of the other local players.

During these finally dry, golden days of spring, Newton postmen were delivering graduation party invitations by the thousands. We got six during the rain week—Julia, Dani, Gabe, Kayla, Benjamin, and Nick. The invitations were all pretty staid and most insisted "no gifts please." Competition for attendance would no doubt be fierce. In 1971, I was mandated to return home after graduation ceremonies, where my parents played host to an impressive collection of aunts and uncles who came to Groton to celebrate my passage from high school. Diary entries indicate I received an impressive stack of envelopes containing $5 and $10 bills; I'd gotten a $50 gift from my godmother, Annabelle. That translated to $500 in today's market, an impressive demonstration of love and support from my favorite aunt.

We were planning a dual celebration for Sam and Alexis. On the glossy invite, Marilou juxtaposed two photos: one featuring the boys at 6 years old, arm and arm, after a soccer conquest; the other from high school with Sam and Lex in the same formation, ten or more years later. I suggested a caption contest for the cover and party invitees were free to check one of the following: 1. Separated at birth, 2. Two guys with great hair, or 3. Brothers from another mother.

The invitations went in the mail on the best day of Alexis's life—the day he got into the University of Massachusetts at Amherst. The day he received his letter, Lex and I went to a reception for U-Mass big shots in downtown Boston, where they congratulated him on his admission and offered to help steer him through the landmines of financial aid, orientation, work-study, and housing. Alexis's family was over the moon. He was going to be the first member of his family to attend college directly after high school. He'd already won an $8,000 scholarship, and one of the North housemasters whispered to me that he was in line for a big award on graduation night.

I was working on an Alexis-Sam piece for the Living section of the *Globe*, something that would maybe give a boost to the much-maligned Metco program. I interviewed both boys, getting the usual monosyllabic answers, except when Sam said, "All I remember is that we met on the day before the first day of kindergarten, and Lex had this really high voice and he had a high-top 'fade' haircut. Also, he loves condiments more than any person on the planet. Mustard, ketchup, hot sauce, you name it."

The next day, Alexis left a school essay on my desk, suggesting it might have some comments I could use for the story. He wrote, "Without Metco, who knows what my life would be like. Statistically, I'd either have dropped out of school, died, or ended up in jail. When I look at some of my friends in Boston, some are in jail, two or three dead, and many have dropped out of school because of motivation and/or having a baby. I refuse to be another statistical black male and I plan to be successful and break down barriers in my lifetime."

Our Kate flew to Ireland right in the middle of all this. As part of her course load at Boston University, she'd committed to a two-month work-study in Dublin, and this meant leaving her team of frizzy-haired freshmen and missing Sam's final days of baseball and high school. This hurt. Kate had been the ultimate big sister for Sam, and I knew he was going to miss his touchstone sibling.

The Tigers went to Framingham on Saturday, May 20, to face Pat Connelly, a control artist who'd walked only a handful of players in his entire varsity career. He'd been scouted by the big league bird dogs in the spring of his senior year, and he put an 0-4 collar on Sam over the first eight innings. James Greeley got the ball for North, his thirteenth appearance in the Tigers' sixteen games. With his future college coach (from the Massachusetts College of Liberal Arts) looking on, and his mother prowling the perimeter like a burglar, Greeley pitched the first eight innings without allowing an earned run. Framingham led 3–1 when the Tigers came to bat in the top of the ninth. North rallied, tying the score at 3–3, and setting up Sam to face a reliever with the bases loaded and two out. Facing a kid who'd struck him out three times in April, Sam fell behind 0-2. As ever, he worked the count to 3-2, then hit a laser double into the gap in right-center, scoring all three runs. Greeley got the side in order in the bottom of the ninth and his mom, Cheryl, was crying after the final out. She said she was thinking about her dad, an affable old man who always sang in the stands during the games. He'd died just before the start of the season and all the players went to his wake.

"I wish he could be here to see this," she said. "I wish he could have seen senior year."

James Greeley's heroic deeds were too quickly forgotten. The bus left without him.

"We forgot Greeley," Sam admitted the next day. "We were all on the bus having fun, talking about the game, when Alex Lee's phone rang. It was Greeley. He was still at the field. I guess he got a ride. Pretty funny."

There was a team dinner at Coach Donnellan's house that Sunday night. There were only four days of classes left for these knuckleheads. We were truly nearing the finish line. That's why I was so relaxed when the phone rang just after 7 P.M.

"Dad, I was in a car accident."

We'd had this conversation earlier in the school year—a late-night episode that turned out to be pretty harmless. This time there was a little more urgency in Sam's voice.

"Are you okay?" I asked.

"Yeah," he said. "I had Nick and Max with me. We're all okay. I think somebody might have been hurt in the other car, though."

"Where are you?"

"The corner of Washington and Lowell."

"I'll be right there."

I could see the ambulance and the blinking lights about a quarter mile before I got to the scene. When I pulled over, the EMTs were putting a woman—wearing a neck collar—into the ambulance. It was still light outside, a nice spring night after some late afternoon thunderstorms.

I recognized both EMTs. One coached the Babe Ruth Cubs in Newton, and he'd ordered Sam intentionally walked several times (his greeting to Sam at the scene was "You can hit homers, but you can't drive"). The other EMT was the son of a woman who babysat for Sarah and Kate when they were infants. I'd given this guy a pair of Larry Bird's sneakers when he was a little kid. The police officer was Paul Marini, and it turned out he went to Newton North with the brother of the coach who'd just hosted the team dinner. Newton's got more than 80,000 people, but this felt like a crash scene from Martin's Pond Road in Groton.

The cop was clearly on Sam's side. He told Sam it looked like it was the other car's fault. Our Toyota Camry looked like P. T. 109. The back right wheel was almost knocked off. It was going on the disabled list, maybe even longer than Big Nick Wolfe.

"I didn't even see the guy until just before he hit us," said Sam as the tow truck took the car away. "He never even hit his brakes. Wolfie saw him first and yelled, 'Oh, shit!'"

This concluded quite a week for Wolfie, AKA "Fatboy." He was still on crutches from his Wednesday's base running mishap, still waiting for results of the MRI. Now this.

Thirty-five years earlier, I'd been in the back seat of Barry Cunningham's red Volkswagen Beetle when we were hit by an onrushing car while Barry tried to execute a left turn. Back then, I'd been the one to alert all passengers of the imminent impact. I remember yelling, "We're gonna get hit," just before Mr. E. Eddie Edwards torpedoed the side of Barry's car. Barry's two-door was a one-door after that day.

Sam went to work on the accident report that night. Applying his senior physics theories, he figured out how many feet the guy traveled in the two seconds he'd needed to execute the turn.

The next morning Newton North was ranked number twelve and Sam was named "Player of the Week" in the *Boston Globe* school sports section.

"Player of the week," I said. "Pretty good. See if you can be Driver of the Week this week."

"Good one, Dad."

June

S AM NEVER SAID ANYTHING about the captaincy, and it wasn't until the final week of the regular season that I learned he'd been reinstated.

"Sam didn't tell you about that?" Coach Siciliano asked me when we were chatting after another shutout masterpiece by J. T. Ross. "We took care of that after the Braintree game. I asked the players if they knew that Sam had lost his captain title and they said no, of course, and I told them—'Well, Sam and I had a little problem, but we're all straight now because Sam is being a good teammate.' They all laughed and said I was just doing it because he'd hit a grand slam that night."

It struck me how different the whole situation would have been with girls. Softball players would have buzzed about the rift between player and coach. There would have been a lot of instant messaging and late-night gossip regarding the touchy situation. Not with guys. High school boys just don't have the maturity and depth of their female counterparts. They think about the next slice of pizza and the next game. There's no time for introspection when you are occupied 24/7 taking care of your own selfish needs.

Captain Shaughnessy and friends had quite a final week of the 2006 regular season. The last games on the schedule coincided with the final days of school for seniors, the spring athletic awards night at North, and the beginning of party and prom season. It was finally warm outside and the smallest event seemed suitable for framing. This was it: the last week of lunch money, the last reminders to get to bed early for a morning test, the last days of parking in third lot and of watching my son from the far side of the chain link fence.

Sam and his classmates observed the annual "Senior Countdown" on the Thursday before Memorial Day. It was their final day of school after thirteen years together, and the 550 members of the graduating class gathered on the long dirty corridor known as "Main Street." Equipped with water balloons, confetti, sparkling water, and all other forms of stupidity and signage, they counted down the final ten seconds of the final minute of the final year. When they got to zero, they trashed the corridor—and one another—then started chanting something original like "Let's get drunk!"

Ah. Good times.

I was sitting on my porch, writing, when Sam and Emily came roaring up to the front of our house in her 1987 white Ford Mercury. Wearing a Golden State Warriors jersey—better to show off those impressive guns—Sam hopped out of the passenger seat, raised his arms toward the sky, and shouted "Victory!" He was smiling. She was smiling. The sun was shining. Emily and Sam reminded me of Brenda and Eddie from Billy Joel's "Scenes from an Italian Restaurant." Bookend ballplayers, a couple of days earlier in their respective baseball/softball victories over Weymouth, they'd both gone 1-3, hitting a triple, and taking a called third strike. Like Sam, Emily was a four-year letterman who'd been called up to the varsity in the middle of her freshman year. Not that we ever asked, but they still claimed to be "just friends," even though they were going to the prom together for the second consecutive spring.

Sam and Emily both had captain duties at the awards presentation at North that same night. These events can be interminable, but I wasn't dreading a moment of it, even though the baseball team was scheduled to appear at the end of the program—after softball, boys' and girls' lacrosse, boys' and girls' track, boys' volleyball, and boys' and girls' tennis.

When the hardball players finally took the stage, I happily noted that they were wearing dress shirts and neckties. No jeans. Stylin' in his shiny pale-blue shirt and white tie, Sam looked like an extra from *Goodfellas,* but I was happy he'd been a ringleader in the baseball team's class act. At the podium, Sam, J. T. ("Captain America"), and James took turns reading their teammates' names. Before closing, Sam summoned his favorite teammate, Big Nick Wolfe, who was still on crutches. Nicky had only recently learned that he was done for the year. He'd torn his ACL on that seemingly innocent base running play in Braintree, and it had taken more than a week for him to get a confirmed reading of his MRI. Sam said, "We want to dedicate the rest of our season to Big Nick, who helped us get this far." Then he embraced his friend. It was a legitimate man-hug, one of those "I love you, man" moments popularized in beer commercials—yet another example of things being better today. Guy teammates never hugged one another in 1971. Someone would have suggested we were "homos."

At the end of the night, individual awards were presented by the athletic department. The final, most-coveted honor was the "Team Above Self" citation given to the boy and girl who pay no attention to personal stats and care only about wins and losses. Needless to say, I was not on the edge of my seat before the male winner's name was called. It's pretty fair to say Sam Shaughnessy will win a Rhodes Scholarship before he'll get a Team Above Self award. The citation went to Jon Laussen, a football/basketball starter who'd done grunt work without complaint for four years.

He'd played in the trenches on the gridiron and took about five shots all season while starting at power forward for the basketball state champs. Laussen was the personification of Team Above Self. Good call by our veteran athletic department.

"Way to go, Chavo," Sam told his classmate after the ceremony.

Chavo. Captain America. Fatboy. Everyone gets a nickname in high school, and sometimes we never even know why. Sometimes they stick. My favorite one in Groton was Jesus Martin. His real name was Dave Martin, and he was several years older than me. He got his lasting nickname because of a flub during an otherwise mundane basketball practice in the mid-1960s. In order to finish practice, the players had to make twenty consecutive lay-ups off the three-man, full-court weave. When they got to nineteen, Dave Martin missed the shot that would have sent everybody home, and a weary, angry teammate shouted, "Jesus, Martin!" From then on, he was Jesus. More than thirty years later, I walked into a bar across the street from the Boston Garden and a young man introduced himself and his dad, saying they were from Groton. I didn't hear the young man when he told me his own name, but when he turned to his dad and said, "This is Dave Martin." I quickly asked, "Jesus—is that you?" The older man smiled and nodded. Still Jesus after all those years.

The Tigers were bused to Wellesley to play crosstown rival, Newton South, at Babson College the day after the awards ceremony. I arrived a half hour ahead of the team and was in my car reading the paper when Sam came off the bus and threw his freshly minted school yearbook at me.

Here's a not-too-surprising confession: I *love* high school yearbooks. I still have all four of my books from Groton and every couple of years I'll sit down and thumb through the pages, reading shallow thoughts that were scribbled by those friends and acquaintances of my youth. I shudder to think of classmates' dusty books scattered across New England, many with yellowed pages marked by my syrupy script from 1968–71. In those days, in my small world, it was a big deal if somebody signed "Love, Alicia," instead of "All the best, Alicia," and I was always looking for clues in those often-forced autographs. There were funny ones, too, of course. When we were seniors and a nervous freshman would ask us to sign his book, we'd write something clever like "I can't begin to tell you about the good times . . . because there haven't been any! Take care, Danny Shaughnessy."

We just killed ourselves laughing with that one.

I still smile when I see one autograph on page sixteen of my senior book. There's a photograph of my favorite janitor (they're custodians now, but they were janitors then), Ray Hickey, leaning against a door frame, left foot on a chair, his thick, calloused hand resting on his knee. His signature is scrawled neatly over his picture. It means something to me now and I like to think it meant something to him then. He was a hard-working guy who kept the gym floor clean and watched our backs and we loved him for it. Hope he knew that.

In the back of my yearbook, there's a passage written by Chris Young, a boy I'd known since seventh grade. Chris and I grew apart during the high school years, and in June 1971 he wrote, "Daniel—It wasn't long ago when you and I were both men of learning. But time has changed that as I'm sure you're well aware. I really appreciate understanding people's lives and people like you have the most strangest, yet something tells me the best. So if you ever get the urge to sit down and talk—Chris."

We never spoke after that and I have no idea where he is now.

That's the nature of those final days of high school. You say goodbye to the most important people you have ever known, the people who went through all the changes with you—and then you never speak to them again.

The theme of Sam's 2006 yearbook was "Look At Me!" It was

as if the Newton North yearbook staff made a conscious decision to validate every *Time* and *Newsweek* theme-issue description of their Echo Boomer generation. "Look At Me!"? Not very subtle. These were the indulged children of boomers, kids who never had to wait for anything, kids who got a trophy just for showing up. They'd been told they were special since they were in cribs, and now they were getting back at us with this hideous message. On page three of the yearbook, the staff explained the theme, stating, "At North you can always find a place where you can stand out by doing what you do best. Be proud of your year at North. Define who you are. Take action to be that person. Relish in your individuality and strengths. You're simply screaming out LOOK AT ME!"

Ugh.

While I sat in the car waiting for Newton North versus Newton South at Babson, I could not resist the urge to thumb through Sam's yearbook and, naturally, I read some of the messages he'd already gathered from classmates. It felt a little bit like peeking at somebody's diary, but Sam didn't seem to be guarding the material. My favorite inscription came from a beautiful young woman named Kayla, who had been Sam's classmate for thirteen years. He'd regarded her as a nemesis back in the early days, calling her "Satan" for a few years. I figured it was the standard guy thing at work—boys act out their secret crushes by teasing the prettiest girls. It's how we avoid true feelings and fear of rejection. Now, in the spring of 2006, Kayla was bound for Duke, and she told Sam, "It's been a pretty sweet thirteen years! So I admit I hated you for a good chunk of it, but you've finally matured into a pretty cool guy. Good luck at BC. I will definitely be seeing you when you play Duke."

North jumped to a 7–0 lead in the first two innings against South. It was North's first game of the season with metal bats, akin to being let out of jail for the hitters. Ryan Walsh hit a monstrous homer in the top of the first, and in the second inning, the South pitcher hit Walsh on the elbow with the first pitch he threw. This provoked some noise from the North bench and for the first time I heard some of our parents say unkind things about rival players. When the rains came in the middle of the second, the game was called off, and they agreed to start over two days hence at the Newton North field.

That night, there was a neighborhood party feting graduates-to-be who had matriculated at the nearby Underwood Elementary School. Some of the former grade school teachers attended and one of them brought workbooks from days when these kids were 6 and 7 years old. There was a slide presentation (Joan Baez's cover of Dylan's "Forever Young" is the standard soundtrack), and photos of our kids as grade schoolers peppered the walls of the giant Victorian home. In every photograph that included Sam, he was holding a bat or ball. My senior son was unusually engaged while thumbing through the aged materials. This surprised me. I'd never thought of Sam as sentimental. Reminded me of me for a change.

Alexis came up to me during the party and said, "I don't know how to feel right now. It's like I'm happy and sad at the same time."

When we got home that night, Sam's black cap and gown (orange tassel) were hanging from the bathroom door behind our hallway entrance. They were the first things you'd see when you came in the front door and they would remain there until the night of graduation.

He left his official school file and his senior writing portfolio on the kitchen counter. The school file includes thirteen years of grades, absentee data, and teachers' comments. Naturally, I still have my file from Groton High School, and it's always fun to re-read what the teachers really thought of me back in the day. Miss Barney, who was young and a certifiable looker in 1971, wrote,

"Dan is somewhat immature (self-conscious) for a senior . . . occasionally becomes nervous and flustered which impairs his performance." Ouch. Then there was this beauty submitted by my well-meaning French teacher, Mr. Lacerte: "In spite of all the effort he put into learning the language, he never truly mastered it. Had he attempted a fourth year, I am sure he would have failed completely."

Thanks, Mr. Lacerte. I'm sure the admissions department at Holy Cross loved that one.

Sam's writing portfolio was amusing and arrogant. The spiral-bound book featured essays he'd written during his years at North, leading with the final paper of his high school years, a two-page ditty entitled "Done." In the first paragraph, he wrote, "I do not care much for analytical writing. I also hate to read. I have managed to not read more than about twenty pages of any book in high school. Pretty impressive I must say. My strategy is nearly flawless. Every teacher will give one writing assignment per book. It is always on a theme or some crap like that. The basic plot is all you need to know, and then look up a few useless quotes."

Not something that needed to be forwarded to the good folks over at Boston College.

The Newton North Tigers went to Natick on Saturday of Memorial Day weekend for their final game in the Bay State League. After parking my car, the first person I saw was Doug Flutie, who had just retired as Tom Brady's backup quarterback with the Patriots. Doug's nephew, Billy, was a pitcher/infielder for Natick, and he was going to Boston College on a football scholarship as a placekicker/quarterback. Doug and I talked a little bit about BC and the Bay State League, then assumed our positions on opposite sides of the Natick field. I'd seen him often in the Patriots locker room during the 2005–2006 NFL season and was ever impressed with how much he cared about the high school exploits of his niece and nephew. He seemed to be the only guy in Boston pro sports who knew more about the Bay State League than myself. It could be argued that he'd become more accomplished and famous than any athlete in the history of Massachusetts high school graduates, yet he was still part of the scholastic culture almost three decades after his glory years at Natick High. Doug's only son, Dougie, is autistic, and the Flutie parents have raised millions of dollars to make life better for other autistic children. Young Dougie's presence at the Natick-Newton game reminded me that I should stop worrying about small things and embrace my family's good health. Nobody gets everything.

Rounding into tournament form, J. T. was at the top of his game and took a no-hitter into the ninth at Natick before allowing a couple of hits and settling for an 8–1 victory. Michael Walsh, the sophomore younger brother of our star third baseman, crushed a homer to left in the middle innings. Dad Walsh walked around to left field to gather the souvenir, his second in two days.

It was late in the season, late in the week, and Natick ran out of able pitchers. This made for an easy day to hit, and I was anticipating Sam's final time at bat when I saw him peeling off his batting gloves and playfully squashing his helmet down on the head of backup first baseman John Michael McGrath. John Michael had hardly played all season, and I was glad Coach Sis was giving him a chance in a game that was clearly in hand. Sam being Sam, I wondered if he'd be annoyed about losing an at-bat against an inexperienced pitcher. John Michael grounded out and finished the game at first base.

"Good game," I said to Sam when I saw him at home later that Saturday. "Were you okay when Sis sent John Michael up to hit for you?"

"That was my idea," Sam said. "John Michael's a good kid. He's worked hard all year."

Wow. So there *was* hope for my son. He did get it. Okay—so he wasn't a candidate for the Team Above Self Award—but at least he'd finally demonstrated some awareness of sportsmanship and fair play. He'd forfeited an opportunity for an average-padding base hit, maybe even another homer, in order to take care of a young guy who'd been riding the bench all year. Maybe it was a reaction to seeing what his sisters went through trying to play Division I softball as walk-ons in a world of stud recruits. Maybe it was something he'd read or heard. I didn't care.

The South game was replayed at North's home field on Sunday, the day before Memorial Day. We had perfect weather and a fairly big crowd for the Newton civil war. Iron Man Greeley got the ball for the final game of the regular season, and he won his sixth game 6–0. Despite the lopsided score, there was considerable tension in the crosstown finale. Sam got into a beef with the home plate ump over a called strike in the first inning. A couple of innings later, he almost got tossed after being called out in an attempted steal of home. He was officially warned by the umpire and so was our head coach. One more word and both could have been banished for the rest of the day—and (state rule) for the next game, which would be the first game of the state tournament. One more ill-chosen word and Sam's high school career could end with a suspension. He could wind up sitting with me in the stands, watching his team eliminated in the first game of the state tournament.

Never one to talk to my son during a game, I went over by the bench where Manny—Sam's crusty, trusted Legion coach—was hanging over the rail.

"Manny, tell him to be careful," I pleaded. "He could lose the tournament."

"We were all thinking the same thing," Assistant Coach Tom Donnellan told me the next day. "We all talked to him. Manny, too."

North's 15-5 record was the best in Coach Siciliano's twenty-year tenure. He'd also won one of the most prestigious teaching awards at the high school. He told me his goal was to win three games in the state tournament. None of his teams had ever moved past the second round.

Sam finished the regular season with a .344 average, 1 homer, and 16 RBIs. He had 15 strikeouts (9 looking), 27 walks, and got hit 4 times. His on-base percentage was .565, but I knew he was disappointed that he hadn't had a dominating season at the plate. People were expecting more after the way his junior year ended and after the manner in which he was recruited. A future Division I player was supposed to do better than that in high school, and I knew he was worrying about the perception that he was overrated.

Never one to coast, Sis scheduled a scrimmage with mighty Boston College High School on the morning of Memorial Day. This would have been unthinkable in Groton in 1971. First of all, our season was always over by the end of May. We never finished over .500 in my three varsity seasons, and even if we had, there's no way we'd have practiced or played on Memorial Day. It was a major holiday in our town. My dad was a Purple Heart veteran, an honored member of the local Legion post, and after years of marching he got to ride in a yellow convertible during the Memorial Day parade. The parade route took my dad right past our home on Hollis Street, and I have fond memories of watching Dad wave from the front seat of the sports car. In my earliest years, the parade was significantly longer because students of Groton School and Lawrence Academy were required to march, en masse, wearing their official school blazers. I liked to think that Groton School grads FDR and Teddy Roosevelt must have marched past my house decades before I was born. In my day, we watched young Peter Gammons walk with his Groton School classmates. By the time I was in high school, Vietnam War protests were in full bloom and the rebellious students of Groton and Lawrence Academy were no longer required to march. The parades were pretty small after that.

The days after "Senior Countdown" were cushy. Sam got to sleep in, then spend the afternoon at baseball practice as he waited for the tourney draw and the end of the rain season. He and Alexis painted the front porch floor in preparation for their graduation party. I kept reminding Sam not to do anything foolish with all this free time and held my breath each night when I shuffled to my bathroom window at 3 A.M., praying that the Acura would be parked in the driveway.

I got a nice e-mail from Emily's mom. Graduation week and the end of the softball season prompted her to dig out a column I'd written when Kate played her final game at North. She wrote, "As I reread it today, I am reminded of how much I dread the end of high school softball, prom, and graduation for Emily (and probably more for myself). The girls managed to land a berth in the tournament and I am spared one more day of the inevitable; the closure of my last baby (my only girl!) finishing school, playing her last competitive softball game, and being part of a team. Softball has been a big part of Emily's life."

The girls won their first tournament game but lost to Lincoln-Sudbury 2–1 in the second round. Newton had a runner on second base with no outs in the seventh (scheduled to be the final) inning when rains came and washed away the rest of the game and the careers of Emily and her senior teammates. The same thing had happened when Sarah was a senior at North. Late in a tournament game, rains made the field unplayable, ending the season. It was the last moment of Sarah's high school career. Sarah and her teammates, soaking wet and muddy—some with big league eyeblack running down their faces—hugged and cried. Then one of them looked out at the field of streams and said, "At a time like this, there's only one thing to do—mudslide!" They gleefully circled the swampy base paths and slid on their bellies across home plate. Many of them would never play competitive athletics again. It was a snapshot of competition, sportsmanship, and the sheer joy of high school team sports.

Sam took Emily some ice cream the night her career ended.

On the first Sunday in June, when most eastern Massachusetts fields were still under water, the Newton North Tigers won their first game of the tournament 14–1, beating Lynn English at the North diamond. This game was played only because Joe Siciliano got up at 5 A.M. and went to the high school with a pump (purchased by the athletic department for $180), a rake, and dozens of bags of Quick Dry. He got help from a couple of players' dads, and by 3 P.M., the field looked pretty good. Sam walked four times and was hit by a pitch before popping up in the eighth inning. He swung the bat only twice all day. He went up to a reporter and joked, "I've got your headline for tomorrow —'Shaughnessy Walks All Over Lynn English.'" By this point, I think I was more frustrated than my son. Ted Williams's mantra "Get a good pitch to hit"—an expression we'd included in our family yearbook tribute to Sam—was becoming something of a joke. There simply were not that many good pitches to hit. The *Globe* said he was getting the "Bonds treatment."

The next day was senior prom. Sam had been hoping the Tigers would play on the night of the prom, rather than on the day after the prom. This was a theory I first heard from Earl Weaver when I covered the Orioles. Baseball's conventional wisdom holds that the most rigorous schedule for a ballplayer is a day game after a night game. Not so, contended Earl: "What's worse is a day game after a day game when you are on the road. That's because you got more time to ruin yourself out on the town after a day game—then you gotta get up in the morning and go play again."

Prom night presented some obvious hurdles. Most of the

players remembered the 2005 tournament, when they played their second-round game the day after the senior prom. It was a mess. Sleepless and maybe hung-over, the Tigers committed eight errors and were beaten 8–1. One of the senior infielders arrived at the field without his glove or his cleats. The senior catcher attempted to play even though he'd been awake for more than thirty-six consecutive hours.

"We had a little meeting about this," Sam told me after practice, while he was getting dressed for the prom. "Guys agreed to try to get to bed by seven in the morning. Nobody's going to stay up the whole time. So we can sleep until about two and play at four. It shouldn't be too bad. I asked Mom to get us a case of Red Bull. That ought to do it."

Prom certainly has changed since I was stepping over cow chips in Joanie McGovern's driveway in 1971. In those days, it cost $25—ten for the ticket, ten for the tux, and five for flowers. Now it's a $70 ticket and a tux rental north of $100. Sam said Emily didn't want flowers. (Softball players are like that. Sarah was a catcher, always bruised, and had a purple welt on her biceps en route to her junior prom. What kind of corsage goes with a hematoma?) Let's not forget the limo cost. I gave my sister 50 cents for gas money to have her boyfriend drive Joanie and me. Now it's white stretch limos, twelve kids to a car. The young ladies are known to spend up to a thousand dollars on dresses, shoes, nails, hair, and tanning appointments. There was some controversy at North this year when one female member of a relay team opted for the prom over the state track meet. Her team was favored to win a state championship, but she spent the night with her date at the Copley Marriott, leaving three junior teammates on the sidelines.

Sis let the seniors out of practice early on prom night. That didn't stop Sam from sweating long after he started pulling on his tuxedo. On humid days, a simple shower doesn't do it for the Shaughnessy men, and Sam had an ice bag on his head as I helped him with his cuff links, vest, and bow tie in front of the full-length mirror on our second-floor stairway landing.

"I'm like you, Dad," he said. "Once I start sweating, I can't stop."

We went to a classmate's home for the traditional mass photo op, and again I was struck at a specific change from thirty-five years ago: in 2006 there were no fat kids, no kids with zits, no slouch-shouldered boys, or moon-faced girls who hadn't yet developed cheekbones. There were at least thirty kids at the photo party and every one was striking. Dads sipped flavored-waters while the moms took photos of the dressed-up kids. I went out to the street and talked to one of the limo drivers—a tough-looking black guy who was smoking a cigarette as he sat in the white Ford Excursion, door wide open.

"High school kids," I started. "This must be some assignment."

"Hey, we were all in high school once," he said.

"You going to keep them on the straight and narrow if they try any knucklehead stuff?"

"Won't be no problems," he said. "Kids are kids. They start anything, I finish it. I fought in the Gulf War, man. This is nothin'."

I felt better. Before going to bed that night, I left a note in front of Sam's door. It read: "Sam, what time do you want me to wake you up for your game?" I left checkmark boxes with choices: noon, 1 P.M., 2 P.M. I knew he had to be at school for the team bus by 2:15.

The next morning at 5:41, I heard the Bulgarian goat bell on our front door and knew that Sam's long night was over. When I passed by his room later in the morning, I looked on the floor and saw that he'd scribbled "1:45" on my wakeup query.

He was awake when I got home just after one in the afternoon and said that prom night went well. Dad did not want any more details. Sam did not appear hung-over, there hadn't been any calls from the cops, and he looked game ready as he sat at the kitchen counter, wearing jersey number 24, eating a turkey sandwich.

I put a little Zevon (always good hitting music) in the disc player as Sam loaded his baseball bag, his tuxedo bag, and the case of Red Bull ("liquid crack" according to Sarah) into the back seat. In something of a regressive development, we were driving Sam to and from school a lot during the final days because we had out-of-town company and a car shortage.

A crew painting the trim on our house wished him good luck as he got into the front seat in full uniform. Like myself, they all wanted to be Sam for the day. We made a quick stop at Mr. Tux and I had a moment when I watched him walk into the shop.

I mean, really. An 18-year-old kid, wearing his baseball uniform, returning his tux on his way to the state tournament the day before graduation? Now *that* is senior year.

We didn't say much on the way to North. I mentioned that the newspaper stats indicated Arlington's pitchers hardly walked anybody all year. He'd be seeing some strikes for a change. I dropped him at the school entrance on Hull Street, gave him the usual dad advice ("Keep your head in and watch the pitch until you hit it"), then drove to Spy Pond in Arlington.

Regardless of your allegiance, you've got to love a place named Spy Pond and a team called the Spy Ponders. The freshwater lake, located off Route 2 leading west out of Boston, is called Spy Pond because there's a lofty perch above the water that served as a lookout for Revolutionary War soldiers who needed to see whether the British were bound for Lexington or Concord. The Arlington High team took on the name early in the twentieth century, and the Spy Ponders had great baseball tradition and an unusual number of elderly male fans who sat in the first base side concrete stands (our moms said those stone seats caused "piles") for just about every game. Spy Pond, I decided, would be an okay place for the end of Sam's high school baseball career.

Coach Sis had scouted Arlington and showed me the mimeographed one-page report he'd handed out to the team. It was thorough. It even said, "Greeley should pick one of their guys off third base."

Cheryl was stalking the premises fairly early. Her James was scheduled to start, making his seventeenth appearance in twenty-two games. His prom date had been Alex Sera, the four-year star pitcher for the North girls and co-MVP of the Bay State League ("What do you think they talked about all night?" quipped Sam). Cheryl said James had left the post-prom party at 3 A.M. to get ready for the start. That sounded good until he booted an easy, two-out comebacker in the first inning. A second error, this one not committed by a prom warrior, gave the Spy Ponders a 2–0 lead.

A couple of hours and eight innings later, it was still 2–0 and Newton had the bottom of the order due up in the ninth. It had been one frustrating day for the Tigers: Ten runners left on base and a lot of hard hit balls right at people. Greeley settled down nicely and picked a Spy Ponder off third in the fifth inning (thanks, Coach), but it looked like the Tigers were going down.

And then we saw some of the high school glory that kids carry with them for the rest of their lives. Led by seniors, the Tigers rallied for four runs in the ninth. Sam tied it with a two-out, two-strike RBI single to left, and Walsh drove home two more to make it 4–2. Greeley got the Spy Ponders in order in the bottom of the inning, and a few parents were crying as they gathered behind the backstop.

Who knew it took Red Bull three hours to kick in?

There were a lot of jokes about not forgetting Greeley this time. I was happy for Coach Siciliano. There was some reward for a man who got up at five in the morning to pump water off his team's home field. This was his best team ever. They were going to the sectional semifinals against St. John's Prep.

I watched the Red Sox and Yankees on television that night. Before going out with his friends, Sam stopped by the TV room and announced that he had not been selected in the first eighteen rounds of the major league draft. The final thirty-two rounds would unfold the next day, graduation day, and Sam said he was hoping to be picked. He was kidding. Sort of. Major league teams are not in a hurry to draft five foot ten high school hitters from the northeast, but a lot of the guys Sam played with in Wilmington were getting calls from the big league ball clubs. One of his summer pro showcase teammates went ninth in the country, which is a $2 million ticket. We both knew Sam's letter of intent to Boston College probably took him out of the mix for the late rounds. Why should a team waste a draft pick on a kid who's already pledged his allegiance to college? Plus, Sam had seen Baseball America's predraft scouting report on him that stated: "figures to be a tough sign with his commitment to Boston College, but he could probably use the college experience anyway. Shaughnessy's short swing generates plus power, but that's his only tool—he's not a strong runner or thrower and lacks a true position."

Sounded a little like Mr. Lacerte's evaluation of my French abilities.

Having nothing to do with the major league draft, I was feeling a little guilty about Sam's situation because that very day I'd learned that Peter Hughes—the man who recruited him to Boston College—was going to take a job as head coach at Virginia Tech. It didn't seem fair to tell Sam this news before his game and everybody was still enjoying the post-victory high after the win, so I kept it to myself a little longer.

It rained the next day, graduation day, and the Newton North

ceremonies were moved indoors to Boston College's Conte Forum. Sam got home from practice just after three and needed to
be at BC by four. Given the hour, normal weekday traffic around
BC, the historic rains, and the friends and family of 550 graduates, this made for a perfect storm of snarled humanity. We
picked up Sam's friend Tom, another thirteen-year neighborhood veteran, and he rode in the back seat with my sister Mary
as we drove two miles to BC through the pouring rain. Sam
was on his cell phone, monitoring the final rounds of the major league draft. "Thirty-nine rounds down. Eleven to go," he announced. I laughed and changed the subject, commenting on the
unlikelihood of all the graduates and their families getting to BC
on time.

"No one knows what's going on," Sam blurted. "I talked to
Gabe and he said people keep calling him."

Gabe was class president, bound for Harvard, a regular at
Chez Shaughnessy. I'd seen his parents on the party circuit all
week and told them how much I was looking forward to Gabe's
speech. I knew he'd come up with something better than my
cornball closing line in 1971, when I took a quote I'd heard on a
popular television show. It went something like this: "First they
came after the Jews, but I was not a Jew so I did not object. Then
they came after the Catholics, but I was not a Catholic so I did
not object. Then they came after the trade unionists, but I was
not a trade unionist so I did not object. Then they came after
me, and there was nobody left to object." The passage had absolutely nothing to do with my speech or with the class of '71, but
I liked it so I used it.

Gabe would do better. I knew.

I dropped my sister and the boys at the front door. Sam and
Tom respectfully stood in the pouring rain while my none-too-
nimble sister got out of the back seat and opened her umbrella.
Mary kept telling them to go ahead, not to wait for her, but they

stalled and got wet while she gathered herself. Mary was impressed and will recite this moment in any future retellings of her experience at Sam's graduation.

Marilou came separately with her dad and Sarah. Uncle Eddie arrived by cab. We sat in section V of the lower bowl and watched the two-hour ceremony unfold. There were boring speeches by a bunch of politicians. Outgoing principal Jennifer Huntington gently reminded us that "in many cultures rain is a sign of good luck."

Gabe did not let us down. He employed one of his dad's tired expressions: "Aim high, finish strong." He said his dad applied this phrase even when encouraging Gabe to take out the trash. Gabe looked great on the Jumbotron scoreboard and he finished strong, but my favorite speaker of the night was a retiring math teacher who was saying goodbye after thirty-six years at North. She complimented the behavior of the class of 2006 during the raucous countdown and at the overnight post-prom party. She said the kids had been respectful of one another. And kind. She also told us that for the first time in her four decades of service—now that she had retired—she suddenly no longer felt like she belonged. That killed me. It was my future, too. I'd no doubt still stop by the school to watch games in days to come, but I would no longer belong in the Newton North stands. I'd be an outsider. A creepy old guy watching other people's kids.

It takes about an hour to announce names and hand out diplomas to 550 kids, and it gets a little tiring once you've seen your child walk the walk. During this lull, after we'd seen Sam get the scroll and the handshake, Sarah's cell phone rang.

"Dad, Sam wants to talk to you," she said, handing me the phone.

I got out of my seat and walked through the portal to the concourse behind the stands, holding the phone to my ear.

"Dad, did I get drafted?" he asked.

Unbelievable. Sam had been a high school graduate for all

of five minutes, and many of his classmates were still in line for their diplomas, and he was calling to ask about the major league draft.

"Sam, I don't think it's happening. Somebody at the paper would have called me if that happened."

We took the perfunctory goofy photos after the ceremony, then went to dinner at the Sheraton, where Marilou's parents were staying.

"No go on the draft," Sam said when I first saw him in the hotel lobby. "I'm kinda pissed."

He was kidding. But deep down I know he secretly had hoped some big league team would pick him in the forty-ninth round. Everybody likes to be able to say they got drafted.

Later that night, there was true disappointment. While I was taking off my necktie and sports coat, Sam came into my office looking wounded.

"Dad, Hughes is leaving," he said.

Welcome to the real world, young man. Less than three hours after you finish school, you get one of those life-lesson kicks in the teeth. The guy who sweet-talked you into coming to his school takes off for greener pastures after getting you to sign a letter of intent. It's an age-old recruiting story.

Sam was confused and concerned. We didn't know who was going to replace Hughes. Sam was hoping for Mik Aoki, the BC assistant who had made the most contact during the recruiting phase.

"Hughes always talked to me about how much he liked my bat speed," he said. "Now . . . I don't know."

I apologized for not telling Sam, but there never seemed to be a good time. I asked him if this gave him any second thoughts about the Notre Dame decision. He raised his eyebrows, grunted, said he was going to Emily's, and walked out the door into the rain.

Ever classy, Coach Hughes called the next day. He told Sam

that Coach Aoki was going to get the job. He said he'd been unable to talk to any of the players or recruits during the process. He told Sam they were going to need hitters at BC next year. He told him how much he liked his competitiveness and that he wished he had had a chance to coach him.

Before the month was over, Notre Dame coach Paul Mainieri left South Bend to take the head coaching job at LSU. Mainieri took the staff with him, including Terry Rooney, the enthusiastic recruiter who'd told all the high school players, "If you just want to be good, go someplace else—if you want to be great, come to Notre Dame!" Turned out Rooney and friends, like Sam, ultimately settled for just being good, not great.

So all those warnings turned out to be true. A recruited athlete needs to pick a school independently of the coaching staff that recruits him or her. The school will still be there in one or two years, but the coach may be gone. Sam batted an amazing 1.000 (two for two) in this game. Both men who'd recruited him were coaching someplace else before the first week of his freshman year. Meanwhile, Sam's classmate Corey Lowe, maybe the best athlete in the North graduating class, switched from Providence to Boston University just before graduation because the Providence basketball staff decided to bring in another guard ahead of Corey. Athletes in North's class of '06 were learning lessons long after the final grades were issued.

The Tigers had been scheduled to play their third game of the tournament the day after graduation, but rain just kept falling. With no prom, no classes, no pomp and circumstance, and no baseball practice, Sam had his first quiet day of the week. I asked him how it felt to have the whole graduation thing behind him.

"It's weird," he said. "We've got practice tomorrow and a game Saturday. Then maybe more games. I just feel like I'm not done yet."

Exactly. It was weird. He wasn't done yet. Same with his parents. There were graduation parties, two a day sometimes. Everywhere we went, other parents were getting all weepy and nostalgic. They were exhaling. But Sam wasn't done. *We* weren't done. Sam was a graduate of Newton North High School and had the orange tassel hanging from the rearview mirror of the Acura, but he was still going to school for practices and on Saturday he'd be getting on a yellow school bus for a ride to Lowell's Alumni Stadium.

It was all about the baseball now. Our youngest child was still a part of the Newton school system, if only for another nine innings. So there was no closure. Not until the final out of the final game.

We had a party for Sam and Alexis on Friday, the night before the big game. The bash had been scheduled for Saturday, but the rain changed the baseball schedule and our party plans. Made me wonder what people do when it rains on the day of their daughter's wedding.

Joe King, Sam's Babe Ruth coach, made it to the party, as did John Colantonio, a Newton firefighter who had coached Sam for three years in Little League. They were the first two guys to draft Sam. John's graduation gift was Sam's old number 7 Indians jersey. Sam's Uncle Bill was in town from Arizona, which seemed like good luck since Bill had been present a year earlier for the three-homer tournament game. Jeremy Kapstein, a Red Sox executive who'd become an unofficial uncle, came late, after the Sox's Friday night victory. Jeremy had also been at the three-homer game.

The cops never came and I was somewhat disappointed. Our DJ played till well after midnight, and there was partying on the porch until after 2:30 A.M., but neighbors of eighteen years do not summon the gendarme when you do this only once a year.

The morning after the party, Sam was out the door, in uniform, with the remaining cans of Red Bull stashed in his bat bag. Naturally, he got rained out again.

"This is so frustrating," he said when he got back to the house.

"Every night I can't go out with my friends because it's a game night, but then there's no game the next day."

I told him it reminded me of the 1975 World Series, the one made famous when Carlton Fisk hit a homer off the foul pole after midnight in the bottom of the twelfth inning. What is often forgotten about that Series is the rain delay, which made a lot of us crazy. The Sox and Reds played Game 5 in Cincinnati on Thursday, October 16, and did not play another game until the following Tuesday. Game 6—the game for the ages—was rained out Saturday, Sunday, and Monday. And then look what happened.

Sam liked this line of thinking.

"That was like Braintree last year," he said. "It rained really hard and a bunch of us were in the Toyota waiting for it to stop and we wrote 'JT Sucks' on the windshield when he walked by. We didn't think we were going to play and didn't really want to play and then I went 0-4 and wished we hadn't played and then I hit the walkoff and it was all good. And for weeks after that, anytime the car would get fogged up, 'JT Sucks' would reappear on the windshield to remind me of that day."

Sunday, June 11—after the senior countdown, the awards night, the graduation ceremony, the Lynn English game, the draft, the BC coach leaving, the monster party, and three solid days of rainouts—the Newton North Tigers finally got a chance to play baseball again. I put Zevon in the CD player and drove Sam to school for the last time.

He'd gone to Emily's on Saturday night with an armful of videos, and I asked what they'd watched. "*Butch Cassidy and the Sundance Kid,*" he said, smiling. "Love that one."

It pleased me that Sam was watching a movie that came out when I was in high school. Self-absorbed and reluctant to grow old, baby boomers believe our generation set the standard for all forms of future entertainment. It has been fascinating to watch three children adopt and embrace so much of the stuff we consumed all those years ago. En route to North, Sam and I traded a few classic lines from *Butch* ("You didn't see Lefors out there, did you?"), and I dropped him at the door.

Two and a half hours later, on a finally perfect, October-like afternoon in Lowell, Massachusetts, the Newton North Tigers took on St. John's Prep in a sectional semifinal. Our guys had won nine in a row and were still on a high from the big victory over Arlington, but I feared we might be overmatched by the Prep, a traditional powerhouse, loaded with 19-year-old kids and future Division I talent.

It felt like a pretty big deal. There was a $7 admission charge, a fair-sized crowd, reporters from at least five papers, and the standard, tinny public address system. Both starting lineups were introduced and we all stood for the national anthem. Sam had a lot of fans on hand—Uncle Bill, two aunts, a cousin from North Carolina, Uncle Eddie, Legion coach Manny, Teo, Sarah, mom, and dad. We gathered with the rest of the Newton baseball community in the stands on the first base side. It was all feeling pretty good after the interminable rains, and we knew the boys were only four victories removed from a state championship.

And then the Tigers came apart like a cardboard box in a tsunami. Newton made five errors. Newton allowed fifteen hits and ten runs. Newton was shut out for the first time all season.

And Newton was no-hit by Steven Peterson, an impressive lefty bound for Marist.

The Tigers had only four base runners all day. Sam got hit by a pitch, struck out on three mighty swings, walked, then came to the plate with one out in the ninth for the final at-bat of his high school career. This was it.

I'd abandoned our big group and found a private spot in the top row, far corner of the first base stands. I just had to be alone. I thought about all the driving and all the games and all the trips to the various fast-food emporiums—Sam eating his double cheeseburger in full uniform. I thought about twelve years of Newton baseball and all the times I had my heart in my throat when he walked to the plate. I thought about the joy. And I thought about how I cared too much and didn't want to let this happen again. This was Sam's life, Sam's game, and he'd do fine with or without me. There would be more strikeouts and maybe some hits in his future, but it was time to let him go and time for me to stop caring so damn much, ever worrying that the happiness of my son was entirely dependent on the quality of his last at-bat.

And then Sam, overswinging madly, hit a 'scuse-me-while-I-kiss-the-sky popup on a 3-1 pitch ("I was going for a home run," he admitted), which was easily gloved by the left fielder. Ryan Walsh followed with a routine fly to center, and it was over for our guys. Sam had his shirttail out and uniform jersey buttons undone by the time Walsh's fly ball settled into the glove of the St. John's Prep centerfielder.

We waited around by the dugout and applauded our boys when they came through the gate, en route to their bus and their final ride home. Sam was the last one off the field and I greeted him with a hug, saying, "Congratulations. That's the end of high school. Not everybody gets no-hit in the final game of their career."

"Pretty special," he said, smiling.

Good irony there. I think.

The thing about high school sports is that if you are on a winning team, it is almost a certainty that you will lose your last game. All the good teams make the tournament and only one wins the championship. This means most kids are going to lose the last one, and the trick is to not make the final game the eternal memory. Sam and his friends seemed to get over this beating fairly quickly. Ten-to-nothing is often easier to take than 2–1. You just tip your hat.

So that was that.

It was time to cancel my subscription to the *Waltham Daily News Tribune*, the local paper that covers Newton High School sports. It was time to cut back on the weekly milk delivery order. It was time to start thinking about home improvement projects for the second floor, which would be empty in a few months. It was time to have Sam gather up those wood bats and put them in storage—he'd be using aluminum in college. It was time for me to turn away from high school sports and get back to my job covering the Red Sox, Patriots, Celtics, and Bruins.

There was one final errand. Sam called me on his cell phone and said he'd be needing a ride home when the bus returned to Hull Street. My well-worn route to Newton North took me past Cabot Field where the Athletics and Cubs were playing a Little League game. Slowing down as I rolled by the ball yard, I saw a dorky-looking man holding a small camera to his eye, leaning over the chain link fence on the first base side.

And I thought to myself, Put the camera away, Dad. You won't need a photograph to remember any of this.

ACKNOWLEDGMENTS

I was lucky to grow up in Groton and owe a great debt to the family friends, neighbors, teachers, and coaches of my little town. And now there is Newton, Massachusetts, another wonderful child-raising city. Thanks to everyone at Newton North High School, particularly athletic department veterans T. J. Williams, Tom Giusti, Bill McAndrews, Christopher Drakos, and Tiz Bailey. Thanks to coaches Joe Siciliano, Tom Donnellan, Walter Birchler, Rob Kane, Rich Barton, Dick Fletcher, Celeste Myers, John Staulo, and Lauren Baugher.

Thanks for once and present bosses Bill Tanton, Dave Smith, Vince Doria, Don Skwar, and Joe Sullivan. Also brother Stan Grossfeld, Kevin Dupont, Stephen Stills, Ken Nigro, Laurel and Wendy Selig-Prieb, Mike Barnicle, Hank Morse, Mike Lupica, Leigh Montville, Tim Russert, Mitch Albom, John Iannacci, John Horn, and Sean Mullin.

Houghton Mifflin editor Susan Canavan kept this going. Thanks also to Megan Wilson, Will Vincent, Sanj Kharbanda, and Beth Burleigh Fuller at Houghton and to Susan, Dave, and the rest of the staff at Skipjacks.

Thanks to all those who gave the manuscript a preread: Sarah Gabert, Christy Lemire, Ed Kleven, Rob Greenfield, Lesley Visser, Suzanne Doria, Eric Monroe, Paul Comerford, Susan Lodemore,

John Lowe, Steve Buckley, Mike Reiss, Eileen Sviokla, Jane Wit, Jane Kenslea, Doris Kearns Goodwin, Jeremy Kapstein, Lenny Megliola, and Doug Richardson. Rick Telander gave me an important kick-start.

Bill Shaughnessy is the original inspiration. Thanks to sisters Mary, Joan, and Ann and my second set of parents, Lou and Mary.

I knew I'd been working on the book too long when I had a dream about playing Little League baseball and found myself in the lefthanded batter's box at Newton's Murphy Field. I bat right. *Sam* bats left. Clearly, it's time to let go.

There would be no book without the collective voices and spirit of the young people who've filled our home with noise and laughter for eighteen-plus years. And as ever, the home team of Sarah, Kate, Sam, and Dr. Marilou took good care of the man at the keyboard in the corner office upstairs.

Dan Shaughnessy
Newton, Massachusetts
September 2006